The Retirement Fingerprint®

CREATING A RETIREMENT PLAN
AS UNIQUE AS YOU

Brian Levy & Shane Brosnan

BML Wealth Management
IRVINE, CALIFORNIA

Brian Levy & Shane Brosnan/BML Wealth Management
18401 Von Karman Avenue
Suite 340
Irvine, CA 92612
www.bmlwealth.net

Book layout ©2013 BookDesignTemplates.com

The Retirement Fingerprint®/ Brian Levy & Shane Brosnan. —1st ed.
ISBN 978-1984118165

Contents

About the Authors vii

Acknowledgments.. xi

Preface 1

Welcome to Retirement, America.................................... 7

Hope for the Best, Plan for the Worst............................ 17

It's Not About the Market, It's About the Math 29

Beware of Hidden Fees 37

What About Taxes.. 51

Getting the Most From Social Security............................ 63

Health Care—the Elephant in the Room 69

Leaving a Legacy 81

Investing Myths and Misconceptions.............................. 93

Eight Investing Mistakes Retirees Make and How You Can Avoid Them 103

The Planning Process—the Way It Should Be Done.................. 129

Dedicated to our BML Wealth Management Client Family

An investment in knowledge pays the best interest.

—BENJAMIN FRANKLIN

About the Authors

Brian Levy is the founder and Shane Brosnan is the partner of BML Wealth Management, which is headquartered in Irvine, California. They engage clients on a fee-basis through a Registered Investment Advisory firm, Cooper McManus. This allows them to act in a fiduciary capacity, the highest standard of care, with their clients. They are comprehensive in their approach and give attention to the five key areas of retirement planning:

- Income Planning
- Investment Planning
- Tax Planning
- Health Care Planning
- Legacy Planning

The offices of BML Wealth Management are located at 18401 Von Karman Avenue, Suite 340, Irvine, California, just across the street from John Wayne Airport.

BRIAN LEVY

BRIAN LEVY originally wanted to be an orthodontist. Somewhere along the line, he learned he would have to administer anesthesia shots to patients and changed course when he was a student at University of California, Santa Barbara, to become a financial professional.

"My first paycheck job was taking orders at the In-N-Out Burger off Inglewood Avenue in Redondo Beach," said Brian. "I earned enough in high school to purchase my first car, a two-door Ford Mustang."

Brian grew up in Torrance, California, and went to West Torrance High School. After graduation, he enrolled at UC – Santa Barbara, where, in 2006, he received his degree in business economics. While in college, Brian interned at an insurance and wealth management firm in El Segundo, California. Upon graduation, he was recruited by several of the large financial firms, but chose instead to work for an independent boutique wealth management and insurance firm, and later branch out on his own to start BML Wealth Management.

Brian and his wife, Ruth, were married Aug. 1, 2010. They have two daughters, Malina and Leila.

"We have known each other our whole lives," says Brian. "We met in kindergarten and our mothers were best friends. I know some people might think it was an arranged marriage, but it wasn't. It just worked out that way."

Brian credits his mother, Diane, who passed away in 2012, with giving him the motivation to succeed at an early age. He received tutoring in business from his father, Larry Levy, who was an executive for Xerox.

"I always knew I wanted to do something in business or finance," he says.

Brian is an avid Los Angeles Clippers basketball fan.

SHANE BROSNAN

SHANE BROSNAN moved to Irvine, California, when he was 3 years old. His parents, Annette and Bill Brosnan, were in the restaurant business, eventually becoming owners of Northwood Pizza, a well-known local eatery. Shane's first job as a fifth-grader was making boxes for delivery.

"I got a penny per box," he remembered. "When I started receiving hourly wages, I made $4.25 an hour and was very happy to get it. My first paycheck was $87 for a week's work."

Shane and his wife, Tiffanny, married in 1996.

"Fate must have brought us together," said Shane. "We met in the third grade, and then, when I was 14, our families lived two houses down from each other."

Shane and Tiffanny are parents of a daughter, Piper, and a son, Beck.

Shane's entry into the business world as a financial professional began when he accepted a position with a financial advisory firm that had helped his parents.

"When I got out of college I thought I wanted to go into sports marketing," recalled Shane. "I went to the interview to appease my parents."

Shane said his parents' financial advisor had helped them invest the proceeds of their business and send three kids to college.

"He asked my parents to have me speak to him first before making any career choices, so I did and decided to give financial planning a shot. The rest is history."

Shane loves to travel when his schedule permits, and is a big soccer fan. He coaches his children's soccer teams and has visited nine English Premier League soccer stadiums.

Shane and Brian became partners at BML Wealth Management when they met one day exchanging mail that had been delivered by mistake.

"We had offices in the same building, and Brian had some of my mail," says Shane. We introduced ourselves and discovered we had the same business philosophy and our professional lives had followed virtually the same path. It only made sense to combine forces instead of compete."

Acknowledgments

Our inspiration for writing *The Retirement Fingerprint®* came from countless meetings and interactions with baby boomers and clients across Southern California. We felt it was important to communicate our message to help people who were in or nearing retirement make better-informed decisions.

It is our hope that this book will inform readers of the steps needed to ensure a successful retirement. Because we are surrounded by uncertainty in our economy, we can't think of a better time to get your financial house in order and have a formal plan to fall back on.

For all of you who bought our book and are reading it, we personally want to commend you for seeking to educate yourself on this complex topic. We encourage you to remain diligent in your quest for knowledge, because the decisions you make in regard to your retirement investments will likely be the most important financial decisions you will ever make.

This book would not have been possible without tremendous support from our team at BML Wealth Management. We are truly blessed to be surrounded by such hardworking and talented individuals.

Most importantly, a project like this cannot be completed without countless hours of research, which meant taking precious time away from our families. It goes without saying, but we want to thank our wives and children: Ruth, Malina, Leila, Tiffanny, Beck and Piper for their love and support throughout this project.

To your retirement success!

~ Brian Levy & Shane Brosnan

Preface

In the wee hours of the morning on Sept. 19, 1910, Clarence and Mary Hiller and their four children were sleeping peacefully in their home in Chicago, Illinois, when Mary was awakened by the sound of footsteps. She found her robe, put it on, and tiptoed to the bedroom door to investigate. The hallway was dark. A gaslight that was usually left burning on low flame had been turned off. Her heart hammering, she returned to her bed and shook her snoring husband awake.

The intruder was Thomas Jennings, a hardened criminal who had been released from prison a month earlier after having served a sentence for burglary. He was now standing at the top of the stairs just outside the children's bedroom. In his pocket was a loaded revolver.

Clarence, his adrenaline surging, saw the shadowy form of Jennings in the hallway and lunged for him as Mary huddled in terror just inside the bedroom door. She heard scuffling sounds, and then three loud bangs. She rushed from the room and saw her husband lying at the foot of the stairs. The intruder had fled through the front door into the night.

Two of the shots Jennings fired had struck Clarence, mortally wounding him. He died just before the police arrived.

About 30 minutes after the shooting, an alert patrolman spotted a man limping down the street just a few blocks from the Hiller's home. The cop asked him where he was going at such a late hour, and what had happened to his leg. While Jennings stammered, more officers arrived on the scene. They searched him, cuffed him and took him to jail for questioning. By this time, the murder had been reported.

Jennings vehemently denied any involvement in the break-in and shooting. Police found evidence the intruder had entered the Hiller home through a window. As luck would have it, the woodwork around the window had been repainted the day before, and the oil-based paint was still tacky. The intruder had left four perfect fingerprint impressions in the fresh paint. It would be his undoing.

Fingerprints were used as seals on documents as early as 1000 B.C., but the concept of using the tiny ridges on the tips of people's fingers to identify them dates to 1686, when a professor at the University of Bologna, Italy, noticed the whorls and loops of the fingerprint formed unique patterns.

The first reported use of fingerprints to solve a crime was in 1896, when an Argentinian woman, Francisca Rojas, left bloody fingerprints on a doorframe after murdering her two children. She tried to place the blame on someone else, but detectives, aware of this new crime-solving technique, used her fingerprints to expose her.

When the fingerprints on the window sill of the Hiller home were compared to those of Jennings, they were a spot-on match. On Feb. 1, 1911, he was tried and convicted of murder and sentenced to life in prison. His attorneys appealed, but the burglar-turned-killer's conviction was upheld by the Illinois Supreme Court. What put him away was not forensic ballistics (they found the pistol on him), as that science had yet to be developed. The indisputable evidence prosecutors needed to prove Jennings had done the deed was based solely on fingerprint identification. Word of the case spread, and police departments in major cities across America began using this new method of identifying criminals by their fingerprints.

Fingerprints, as it turns out, are as unique as humans themselves. Just like snowflakes, no two are exactly alike. Even identical twins, who share the same DNA, have been found to have distinctly individual fingerprints.[1, 2, 3]

Perhaps this will help to explain why we chose *The Retirement Fingerprint®* as the title for this book. Just as there are no two humans alike, there is no one-size-fits-all retirement plan. No cookie-cutter solutions. No silver bullets. If anybody tries to tell you differently, sorry folks—it just ain't so. Retirement plans must be tailor-made—individually fitted to the specific needs and desires of the retiree.

For a case in point, take Joe Average and his neighbor, John Doe. Joe and John live side by side in houses with an identical floor plan. They both own two cars and each has a wife and two kids; all of them are the same ages. While we are in fantasy world here, let's give them identical jobs and make their net worth the same. If Joe and John visit the same financial advisor on the same day of the week to plan for their eventual retirements, shouldn't they have the same plan?

Absolutely NOT!

Why?

Because Joe is not John, and John is not Joe. Unless they have the same values, goals, dreams, desires and identical ideas as to what they want their money to do for them, they will have separate plans and strategies unique to them and them alone.

[1] Swiss Federal Police. Oct. 30, 2017. "The History of Fingerprints." www.onin.com.

[2] Anil K. Jain. Michigan State University. "On the Uniqueness of Fingerprints." http://biometrics.cse.msu.edu/Presentations/AnilJain_UniquenessOfFingerprints_NAS 05.pdf.

[3] Michelle Bryner. Oct. 31, 2012. "Do Identical Twins Have Identical Fingerprints?" http://www.livescience.com/32247-do-identical-twins-have-identical-fingerprints.html.

What Is Money?

When you stop to think about it, money is only numbers. It can be numbers printed on paper, stamped on metal discs or digitized on a computer screen. These numbers contain no intrinsic value—they are merely abstract symbols. The only value they have is what is *assigned* to them. The government may assign a value to currency, but who assigns value to our wealth? *We do!* It's what you DO (or intend to do) with your money that gives it true value. A billionaire may lose $100,000 in the stock market in a single day, and it is pocket change to him. The same loss by a working Joe who has saved all his life to put aside $200,000 means he has lost half his life's savings and will have to dramatically alter his lifestyle as a result. That's why we say wealth is relative.

Everyone's vision of retirement is as unique as a fingerprint.

At BML Wealth Management, we interview hundreds of people each year. A standing question is, *"What do you see yourself doing in retirement?"* The answers vary. Some have similar visions, but none of them are exactly alike.

"We have five grandchildren," said one couple. "We can think of nothing more delightful than getting to know them better and spending time with them. We want to do the same with our great-grandchildren when they come along."

"We both love to play golf," said another pair. "You KNOW where we will be spending our time."

In our conversations with clients and prospective clients, we have encountered still others who intend to turn their hobbies and passions into second careers when they retire.

The point is, different strokes for different folks. With each differing dream and set of values comes a completely separate and distinct retirement plan, just as individual as a fingerprint.

In this book, we will explore five key areas of your financial life, and how your unique retirement plan should interlock with each of them. We will also address the need for planning, and why it is essential that you become proactive in establishing strategies to carry you forward once you reach the age of 50.

We also intend to frankly dispel some myths about retirement planning.

What you won't find in this book are hot stock tips and get-rich quick schemes. If you bought this book hoping to find the next Google or Apple, or some magic market-timing formula, please see us personally and we will be happy to refund the purchase price. The fact is, such quick-fix approaches to financial planning seldom work, and they can even torpedo a long-term retirement plan.

What you will find in the following pages are tried and true methods and strategies that, if properly executed, can lead you to a more confident retirement. If you keep reading, you may also find some concepts that may be new to you, or at least unfamiliar. Please approach these ideas with an open mind. On any journey, some of the most attractive scenery is off the beaten path. Likewise, some of the most effective strategies to preserve wealth and avoid unnecessary taxation won't be the topic of conversation around the office cooler. Nor will they appear in the pages of financial magazines designed to sell you something. Some of the most sensible strategies for building and preserving wealth are well-kept secrets that lie right in front of us, "hiding in plain sight," you might say. You will see what we mean.

Lastly, before you explore *The Retirement Fingerprint®*, let us take this opportunity to thank you for picking up this book, and even further, to commend you for your willingness to expand your knowledge on retirement—the phase of our lives that is appropriately called "the golden years." It can truly be just that for anyone with a desire to put the power of saving and investing to work with accurate knowledge and patience. It is our sincere wish that such is the case for you.

CHAPTER ONE

Welcome to Retirement, America

"I'm going to retire and live off my savings. What I will do the second day, I have no idea."

~ *Unknown*

To officially be a baby boomer, you must have been born between 1946 and 1964. According to statistics released by the Pew Research Center in 2010, baby boomers are retiring at a rate of around 10,000 per day. Some studies say 9,000 per day. Either way, that's a whole lot of people quitting their jobs each day and starting to live off their savings, investments and other sources of income.

To put this retirement tsunami in perspective, we live and work in Irvine, California, located 15 miles from Angel Stadium in nearby Anaheim, home to the Los Angeles Angels. The capacity of that beautiful stadium is approximately 45,000. Imagine that stadium packed to the rafters; about twice that many Americans turn 65 every 10 days or so. America's retirement freeway is getting a little crowded.

In his book, *The Greatest Generation,* journalist and television newsman Tom Brokaw described the generation who grew up during the Great Depression of the 1930s, and then went off to fight World War II. When the boys came home, they shed their uniforms for suits and work clothes and began buying homes and raising families. This led to one of the greatest economic booms in the history of America. The children born to that generation were called baby boomers because of the sudden jump in the birth rate. With each child born after World War II came the need for housing, education, food, clothing and transportation. This phenomenon helped turn the United States into the industrial and commercial giant it is today.

Brokaw also wrote *Boom! Voices of the Sixties,* in which he shares his memories of growing up as a baby boomer in the 1960s.

Brokaw writes: *"Boom! One minute it was Ike, and 'The Man in the Gray Flannel Suit,' and 'The Lonely Crowd.' And the next minute it was time to 'turn on, tune in, drop out.' Time for 'We Shall Overcome' and 'Burn, Baby, Burn.' While Americans were walking on the moon, Americans were dying in Vietnam. There were assassinations and riots. Jackie Kennedy became Jackie O. There were tie-dyed shirts and hard hats, black power and law and order, Martin Luther King Jr. and George Wallace, Ronald Reagan and Tom Hayden, Gloria Steinem and Anita Bryant, Mick Jagger and Wayne Newton. Well, you get the idea."*

Ready for Retirement?

Perhaps no other generation before or since has changed the world as much as these kids who grew up watching *Leave it to Beaver* and *Father Knows Best* on black and white TV, gave us rock 'n' roll, and saw men walk on the moon.

Demographers—people who study the characteristics of human population—tell us no other generation in history created more wealth and more debt at the same time. As boomers were growing up, the capitalist world was awash with stuff to buy—automobiles, color TVs, stereos, electronics. They couldn't get enough of America's "horn of plenty." Their conservative parents, still smarting from the privations of the Great Depression, tended to save up for what they wanted. Not boomers. They invented credit cards. This made it possible to buy now and pay later.

According to NerdWallet, an organization that tracks personal finance data, debt has now become a way of life for Americans. As of 2016, the average American household owed $16,016 in credit card debt, $172,806 in mortgage debt, $28,535 in automobile loans and $49,042 in student loans.[4]

Recent studies show boomers are increasingly entering their retirement years saddled with debt. The Money section of U.S. News & World Report revealed "the share of adults age 65 and older with debt increased from 30 percent in 1998 to 44 percent in 2012," and "24 percent of older adults continue to make mortgage payments in retirement, up 16 percent from 1998."[5]

Living Longer

There is no doubt people are living longer. According to the Urban Institute, a research organization that tracks and analyzes census figures, "between 1920 and 1980, life expectancy at birth increased 17 years for men and 14 years for women." The analysis concludes men turning 65 in 2030 can expect to live six years longer than those who turned 65 in 1970. Over the same period, women's life expectancy at age 65 increased four years.

---

[4] Erin El Issa. 2016. "2016 American Household Credit Card Debt Study." www.nerdwallet.com/blog/average-credit-card-debt-household.

[5] Emily Brandon. US News & World Report. Feb. 12, 2016. "5 Baby Boomer Retirement Trends." https://money.usnews.com/money/blogs/planning-to-retire/articles/2016-02-12/5-baby-boomer-retirement-trends.

That's all good news, isn't it? Well, yes and no. As the UI report notes, "One consequence of this increased longevity is that retirement savings will have to last longer."[6]

Guess what is the greatest fear shared by aging baby boomers? If you said spiders, snakes or heights, you would be wrong. It's *running out of money in retirement.*

"Older Americans' No. 1 fear about their retirement is that they won't have enough money to afford retirement," writes Catey Hill, an editor with *MarketWatch,* a financial website owned and operated by Dow Jones. Hill cites a survey conducted by the Transamerica Center for Retirement Studies, which reported approximately 43 percent of those interviewed said their greatest fear about retirement was outliving their savings and investments. This fear surpassed such other fears as loneliness, boredom, declining health and even death.

Hill also cited a survey released by the American Institute of CPAs, where 57 percent of financial planners said, "running out of money was the top retirement concern for their clients." She added the financial firm Allianz reported "more than six in 10 baby boomers feared running out of money before they died more than death itself."

Looks like we can add longevity to the list of potential retirement pitfalls.

Ironically, when Social Security was introduced in 1935, American life expectancy was just over 59 for men and just above 63 for women. Since the eligibility age was 65, this means the average American would never live long enough to collect benefits.

---

[6] Richard W. Johnson, Karen E. Smith. Urban Institute. Feb. 9, 2016. "How Retiring is Changing in America." https://www.urban.org/features/how-retirement-changing-america.

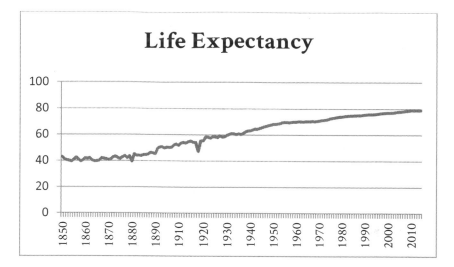

How times have changed! Now, with the ratio of workers paying into the system to those collecting benefits steadily decreasing since 1950, and expected to decline into the future, it's no wonder people are questioning the viability of the program.[7]

Endangered Social Security?

Even the Social Security Administration acknowledges the system must change if it is to still be here in future decades. A paragraph on the front page of a sample Social Security Statement bearing the date of Sept. 5, 2007, contained the following warning paragraph:

"About Social Security's Future: Social Security is a compact between generations. For decades, America has kept the promise of security for its workers and their families. Now, however, the Social Security system is facing serious financial problems, and action is needed soon to make sure

[7] Allianz Life of North America. 2016. "Rethinking What's Ahead in Retirement." https://www.allianzlife.com/-/media/files/allianz/documents/ent_1154_n.pdf

the system will be sound when today's younger workers are ready for retirement.

In 2017, we will begin paying more in benefits than we collect in taxes. Without changes, by 2041, the Social Security Trust Fund will be exhausted and there will be enough money to pay only 75 cents for each dollar of scheduled benefits. We need to resolve these issues soon to make sure Social Security continues to provide a foundation of protection for future generations."

The Disappearing Pension

Times were in America, you worked 40 or so years for a company and retired with a gold watch and a substantial portion of your salary, called a pension. Every month, for the rest of your life, you could count on a check appearing in the mailbox. That income, plus your Social Security, was primarily what you retired on. Add to that your personal savings, and you had what was called "the three-legged stool" of retirement.

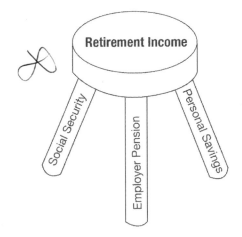

Now, with Social Security threatened and pensions having become an endangered species, to say the once-sturdy three-legged

Good Story

stool of retirement has become a bit shaky is understating the case. The only leg you can really depend on is your personal savings, and if you don't manage that correctly, you could find yourself flat on your... Well, you could find yourself without a leg to stand on.

What happened to pensions? You could say they have gone the way of the Studebaker. If you are a baby boomer, you probably remember the Studebaker. Back in the 1950s, it was one of the most popular cars on the road. It was fast, sleek, and in many ways ahead of its time in terms of design and performance. They were the first car to have seatbelts and padded dashboards. The Studebaker Corporation was named for John M. Studebaker, a wagon maker who began making electric cars in 1902. He introduced gasoline-powered models two years later. Studebaker was generous with his employees and times were good. But the 1960s weren't kind to Studebaker and, by the middle of the decade, the automaker was in financial trouble. The last Studebaker rolled off the assembly line on March 16, 1966.

So, what does all that have to do with pensions? When the company began closing plants and sending workers home, corporation executives realized their pension plans were too generous and they would not be able to keep their word. Thousands of laid-off workers either got nothing or had their payouts reduced drastically. The auto workers fought back. Their unions complained loudly to Congress. The chorus was soon joined by other workers whose companies had defaulted on their pension commitments.

On Sept. 12, 1972, NBC television broadcast a special report, *The Broken Promise,* exposing poorly funded pension plans and the negative effects they were having on American workers. Next came a Congressional investigation and public hearings. In 1974, Congress passed the Employee Retirement Income Security Act, also known as ERISA, a federal law that would make employers toe the line when it came to pensions. Companies offering pensions would now have to make full disclosure of how they were investing pension fund assets. If they didn't, they would be breaking the law and have to answer to the courts. However well-intentioned, it was the beginning of the end for guaranteed pension programs.

Enter the IRA

What took the place of pensions was a by-product of the ERISA legislation—a new retirement instrument called the individual retirement account, or IRA.

This new law provided that a taxpayer could contribute a portion of his salary to an IRA ($1,500 per year in 1975; $5,500 per year in 2018 with an extra $1,000 allowable for earners over age 50), and reduce his or her taxable income by the same amount. This new tax-advantaged IRA also allowed the saved money in the account to grow tax-deferred. You would not have to pay taxes on the money until you withdrew it. What a sweet deal, right? Since no taxes were coming out as the account accrued interest, the compounding was accelerated. Your interest earned interest, and the interest on the interest earned interest.

Enter the 401(k)

Then, in 1978, Uncle Sam made the 401(k) possible. This new savings vehicle that sounded a lot like a breakfast cereal was named after a section of the Internal Revenue Code and now allowed employers to offer employees a tax-advantaged retirement savings program. "Defined-contribution plans" (401(k)-type programs) were now replacing "defined-benefit plans" (pensions) as the retirement program of choice among employers. Why not? The burden of saving for retirement now lay squarely on the employee. Even if the employer offered generous matching funds (many of them did, and some of them still do), the onus remained on the employee to save.[8]

Good old Uncle Sam! Right? Don't forget, tax-***deferred*** is not tax-***free.*** Uncle Sam will get his slice of a much bigger pie later, assuming the saver's investment choices are good ones and the account grows.

Are 401(k)s a good deal? They can be, of course. If your employer offers matching funds, that's free money! You can take advantage of it by contributing the maximum, at least up the match. Regular, steady contributions over several years to a 401 (k) program can provide a handsome income in retirement. But a few words of caution:

- You must make investment choices within the program. These are usually stock-market-based options, typically mutual funds. As you approach retirement age, it is wise to be conservative in these choices. During the stock market crash of 2008, some who were on the verge of retiring and had not adjusted their risk saw their 401(k) balances slashed in half.
- Understand there is a measure of risk with any stock market investment.
- Understand "education" provided by the custodians of the plan is not necessarily good investment advice for retirement.
- Understand there are investment costs associated with the plan.
- Avoid investing in too much company stock (remember Enron).

---

[8] Roger Lowenstein. Wall Street Journal. Oct. 1, 2013. "The Long Sorry Tale of Pension Promises." https://www.wsj.com/articles/the-long-sorry-tale-of-pension-promises-1379723751.

- "Cashing out" a 401(k) can be very costly and create unnecessary taxes. Rollovers are much preferred.

There's an old saying, "If it is to be, it's up to me," meaning you must make intelligent choices in life to be successful.

When things go wrong, it is easy to blame others for our difficulties, but the happiest and most successful people in this world are those who are proactive and accept responsibility for their futures.

Yes, that three-legged stool of retirement is getting wobbly and unreliable. While Social Security will most likely still be around for the baby boomers, it may not be for their children—at least not in its present form. Even so, living just on Social Security puts most people at the poverty level. It may help a little, but it's not enough.

Pensions? Well, we've covered that. If you have one, consider yourself one of the fortunate few. Retirement programs such as 401(k)s are great, but you must manage them carefully, especially as you near retirement.

That leaves personal savings and wise investment. Please repeat after me, retirees and soon-to-be-retirees: "If it is to be, it's up to me." This goes for separating fact from fiction, sifting financial fantasy from financial reality, and making wise choices with your wealth.

Hope for the Best, Plan for the Worst

"Expect the best, plan for the worst, and prepare to be surprised."
~ Dennis Waitley

The dark, icy waters of the North Atlantic were as smooth as glass on the night of April 24, 1912 when the RMS Titanic, her captain and crew, unaware of her surroundings, sailed full steam into a dangerous field of icebergs.

At 11:40 p.m., the ship's lookout frantically yelled the fateful words, "Iceberg right ahead!" In less than three hours, the ship would be in two pieces, tumbling into the inky fathoms, and would finally come to rest on the ocean floor two miles below. On board were 2,224 souls. All but 710 would perish.

Twenty-five minutes after the collision, Captain Edward J. Smith knew his ship was doomed. The iceberg, which was mostly under the surface of the water, was 10 times the mass of the ship. It had ripped open a 230-foot gash in her hull. At 12:05 a.m., the captain gave the order to lower lifeboats, telling his crew to take the women and children first. It soon became apparent the unthinkable was happening to the "unsinkable."

Adding to the tragedy was the fact that the enormous ocean liner was not carrying enough lifeboats. The ship was built to carry 32 lifeboats, each with a capacity of 70 passengers. Sadly, there were only 20 lifeboats aboard. The White Star Line felt having any more lifeboats would clutter up the deck and obstruct the view of the ocean. To make matters worse, many of the 20 lifeboats were deployed only partially full.

In 1912, the organization that oversaw safety at sea was England's Board of Trade. The number of lifeboats a vessel was required to provide was based not on passenger count, but on the ship's gross tonnage. Regulations had not been updated since 1894, when ships weighed far less than the Titanic.

But the biggest culprit in the lifeboat shortage was overconfidence and lack of preparation. The "unsinkable" handle had been given to the Titanic because she was made of the finest steel that could be manufactured at the time, and had a double bottom and 15 sections that could be closed off in the event of a breached hull. An air of arrogance over the ship's invincibility was exhibited by the White Star Line from the top down. Even the wireless operator aboard the doomed ship ignored several warnings about the iceberg field and did not report them to the captain.[9, 10, 11]

Misplaced Confidence

Economically, too, anything can happen. As we write this book in 2017, the memory of the stock market crash of 2008 and the ensuing Great Recession is fading. But, for those investors who

[9] Ultimate Titanic. 2012. "The Sinking." http://www.ultimatetitanic.com/the-sinking/.

[10] History on the Net. Aug. 5, 2014. "The Titanic – Lifeboats." www.historyonthenet.com/titanic/lifeboats.htm.

[11] Capital Steel & Wire, Inc. "Steel of the Titanic." www.capitalsteel.net/news/blog/steel-titanic

lost as much as half their life savings, it is still fresh in mind. Many who were caught in that financial crash have yet to recover. Not that the economy hasn't recovered; it has. As we write this, the stock market is on a roll. On Jan. 4, 2018, the Dow Jones Industrial Average hit and exceeded 25,000—a landmark event for Wall Street—and optimism is running in the streets of lower Manhattan like a flash flood.[12]

So why were those who lost half their life savings in the 2008 crash unable to fully recover their losses?

Timing.

The financial crisis struck·many just as they retired, or were on the verge of retiring. They were at a point where they would have to begin relying on their investment accounts for income and could not participate fully in the market's recovery.

Hindsight vision is 20-20, of course. Apparently, too few saw the 2008 financial crisis coming, but we can now see the causes clearly. Banks were too loose with mortgage loans. Major banks that were "too big to fail" were propping up the market with something called "credit default swaps," which made the entire economy into a house of cards. The mortgage loan "chickens" came home to roost in 2007 when the housing bubble burst. Too-big-to-fail banks were suddenly forced to beg the government for bailouts. The rest, as they say, is history.

If you see a similarity between what happened on Wall Street in 2008 and what happened with the Titanic 1912, you are not mistaken. Overconfidence and arrogance were involved in both tragic scenarios.

Individual investors were taken unawares. They either misread the risk of the market, or placed their trust in an advisor who did.

---

[12] Corrie Driebusch, Michael Wursthorn and Georgi Kantchev. The Wall Street Journal. Jan. 5, 2018. "Dow Industrials Cross 25000 for First Time." https://www.wsj.com/articles/global-stocks-extend-gains-1515034296.

compare the similarities between the Titanic & 2008. Arrogance, misplaced confidence

"Our broker didn't warn us something like this could happen," said one woman. She and her husband, whom we shall call the Smiths, were owners of a successful import-export business. Over the years, they had invested in their business, plowing profits back into its manufacturing center. They employed 14 people and had a sales staff of four. On Sept. 29, 2008, when the Dow plunged 777 points in a single day, he was 65 and she was 64 years old.

The Smiths had personal savings. They had $940,000 in a brokerage account. They didn't worry about this money because, according to their broker, they were "diversified."

The Smiths had planned to work until the end of the year. Then, they would turn over the business to their son and his wife. They would continue receiving a small salary from the company. That, combined with their Social Security and income from their brokerage account would enable them to retire comfortably. They intended to travel and do some of the things they had always dreamed of.

But by the end of November 2008, their $940,000 nest egg had been reduced to just over $500,000 and was sinking daily. Their plans were wrecked.

"We should have paid more attention," said the husband. "We were so busy taking care of the business, we just gave no thought to the details of our personal finances. We just put ourselves in the hands of our broker and thought we were taken care of."

"Our broker told us to just hang in there," the wife said. "He told us we were not alone, that all boats go down with a falling tide. But this wasn't just a falling tide—the entire *ocean* disappeared!"

As things turned out, the couple had to regroup financially and postpone their retirement. They worked another five years. This time around, they were much more careful with their nest egg and made more conservative choices to avoid a repeat of their 2008 experience.[13]

Three Financial Phases

What blindsided the Smiths was failure to understand the financial phases of life and invest accordingly. Those phases are:

- Accumulation
- Preservation
- Distribution

The *accumulation* phase begins when you are just starting out in life. You exit your education and enter a career, and then perhaps move on to buying a home and raising a family. As an investor, you are focused on building your assets. Your tolerance for risk is higher. Because time is on your side, you can ride the ups and downs of the stock market with impunity. This is the time to save and invest aggressively.

The *preservation* phase is the mid-cycle. You have worked hard, saved hard and invested diligently. Retirement isn't here yet, but it's on the horizon. The bulk of your working life is in your rearview mirror, but you have a few years to go before you can leave the job behind and retire. For most people, this period begins in their 50s. Your income and your net worth is much higher than it was when you started out in life. You have worked hard to build your retirement nest egg, and you want to protect it. You need growth to continue, but you also need downside protection.

The *distribution* phase begins after you retire. Once severed from your umbilical paycheck, you will be living on your other

---

[13] Kimberly Amadeo. The Balance. April 3, 2017. "Stock Market Crash of 2008." https://www.thebalance.com/stock-market-crash-of-2008-3305535.

sources of income, and you need it to last the rest of your life. During this phase, you are interested in growth with safety and conservative strategies. When it comes to stock market investments, time is not on your side. You are more risk averse now because your resources are finite and your capacity to produce is diminished. Predictability and guarantees are your financial watchwords during this phase.

The Rule of 100

One enduring investing guideline is the Rule of 100. It is a "rule of thumb," not a hard and fast rule. Take your age and subtract it from 100, and that's the approximate percentage of your assets that may be invested with a reasonable degree of risk. The rest should be protected from loss. Another way to calculate it is to place a percent sign after your age, and that's the percentage that should be kept safe. The rest can be invested with a reasonable degree of loss.

Rule of 100

100 - your age

Ex: 100 - 65

35 ← your

ballpark

acceptable risk

The Rule of 100 has replaced the "4 Percent Rule" as an investing guide. Following it is like having an investing guardrail on the side of a curvy mountain road. It may restrict us somewhat, but it keeps us out of danger.

The Outdated "4 Percent Rule"

After the 2008 stock market crash and the Great Recession that followed, most financial advisors waved goodbye to the "4 Percent Withdrawal Rule." It was based on a formula that no longer worked. How did the "4 Percent" theory ever become a rule in the first place? It's an interesting story.

William P. Bengen, a California financial planner in the early 1990s, was crunching numbers and running projections to determine what percentage of a brokerage account a retiree could safely withdraw and not run out of money for 30 years. Using the market data he had on hand, he tinkered with differing rates of withdrawal, as well as varying methods of allocation, until he came up with 4 percent.

The *Journal of Financial Planning* published Bengen's research in an article titled, "Determining Withdrawal Rates Using Historical Data." The magic number actually turned out to be 4.5 percent, but was dubbed the "4 Percent Rule" by Wall Street. Bengen's idea was to periodically re-balance the portfolio to contain 60 percent stocks and 40 percent bonds and allow the amount withdrawn to reflect a 4.15 percent annual inflation rate over the years.

It sounded great. Especially to the brokerage community. They heartily latched onto Bengen's formula and made it the Holy Grail of retirement income planning.

There was nothing wrong with Bengen's research. The math worked. So, what went wrong? Bengen crunched his numbers at a time when the stock market was soaring and appeared to have no ceiling. This was before the tech bubble burst in 2000, and before the financial crisis of 2008. The decade after 2000 is called the "lost decade" by many in the investing community because, for all the ups and downs of the market during these years, there was no appreciable gain.

People in the software community have an expression, "garbage in, garbage out." In other words, if the premise on which a formula is based is flawed, then the application of that formula will be flawed as well.

An article titled, "Say Goodbye to the 4% Rule," written by Kelly Greene appeared in the March 1, 2013, issue of the Wall Street Journal. It included the following paragraph, which showed how flawed the 4 Percent Rule became when projected over the numbers generated by Wall Street after 1999:

"If you had retired Jan. 1, 2000, with an initial 4 percent withdrawal rate and a portfolio of 55 percent stocks and 45 percent bonds rebalanced each month, with the first year's withdrawal amount increased by 3 percent a year for inflation, your portfolio would have fallen by a third through 2010, according to investment firm T. Rowe Price Group. And you would be left with only a 29 percent chance of making it through three decades, the firm estimates."

21st Century Investing

Investing strategies should have an expiration date stamped on them like cartons of milk. What worked when we were in our accumulation years won't work when we approach retirement. With each phase of our financial lives, we must rethink our strategies to keep them viable and keep us on track to achieve our goals.

When we approach retirement, our mission is to preserve and protect our resources to create an income that will sustain us for the rest of our lives in retirement. Timing is just as important in investing as it is in farming.

Hustle-bustle, population-packed Southern California is also home to several large farms. Just a few miles south of our office is Tanaka Farms, a 30-acre family-owned operation that has been growing fruits and vegetables since 1940. You can count on their market stands to appear every February, laden with produce for sale.

Glen Tanaka and his wife, Shirley, the farm's current owners, are hands-on farmers who can tell you timing is very important in what they do. There is a time to plant each crop they grow with very little margin for error. There is also a time to water, fertilize and harvest. There is a time to store seed and preserve it during the off-season.

It's the same with investing. We must change tactics when the investing purpose changes. Bengen's 4 Percent Rule formula may have been flawed, but his mission was right on—turn your investment account into a dependable income for life. His idea would have worked had the stock market continued to be monodirectional (up). But the experiment should be glaring evidence that a formula rooted solely in the stock market can never offer guarantees.

Does that mean it can't be done? No. One way to do it is through a concept known as "laddering"—dividing your assets into income-generating time categories. The idea here is to generate a paycheck without dramatically erode your principal.

How long will you live in retirement? That is X, the unknown, isn't it? But from an actuarial viewpoint, if you are in good health your chances are excellent that you will live at least 20 years in retirement. The way longevity works, the longer you *have* lived, the longer you *are likely to* live. According to the Society of Actuaries (SOA), a 65-year-old-woman has a 50/50 chance of living another 20 years to age 85. The SOA's online calculator indicates a 65-year-old man has a 50/50 chance of living to age 82. When you read the "average life expectancy in America is 81," you may not realize that considers life expectancies from birth. That doesn't apply to someone who has already reached age 65. If that is you, chances are very good your retirement could last for 30 years or longer.[14]

Should We Care About Inflation?

Bengen's 4 Percent Rule was careful to figure in inflation. It's a shame it didn't work. Should we worry about inflation?

Inflation is not so much a green-eyed monster that comes out of its cage in a rage as it is a slow-growing parasite whose effect is almost imperceptible but pervasive. When we read the average annual inflation rate is 3.22 percent, it doesn't sound too bad. A loaf of bread that cost $3.00 this year will set us back $3.10 next year. Big deal. But at that rate, prices will double every 20 years. If

---

[14] Steve Vernon. MoneyWatch. Oct. 16, 2014. "How much longer might you live? Think again." www.cbsnews.com/news/two-common-mistakes-we-make-thinking-about-how-long-we-might-live.

you look back at what stuff costs, you can see that is about what has happened.

Inflation doesn't stop when we retire. Let's say you establish you can live on $80,000 per year, and you pull the trigger on your retirement when you reach the point where you can reasonably expect that from your income sources. Does your retirement plan take inflation into account? Will your income sources pump out $160,000 per year 20 years later?

Think about how much it cost you to do something simple like go to the movies when you were a kid. How long ago was that, and now what does it cost? The same goes for the price of transportation, housing, medicine, food and everything else your money must provide in retirement.

So, no, we can't ignore inflation. It erodes your savings and will make it difficult to live on a budget. A financial advisor who doesn't incorporate it into retirement income planning is either blind or irresponsible.

Inflation is also an unknown factor. All we know for certain is history. Inflation is a factor in producing a lifetime income. You may establish a strategy for producing an income, but if that income comes up short, then you have aimed too low. The challenge is to guarantee an income that is both long lasting and compensates for the steady pressure of inflation to erode the buying power of the dollar. The last thing you want to do is lock into an income stream, only to find out 10 or 15 years hence that it can no longer support your lifestyle. What would you do then? Returning to work is one option, true. After that long a layoff, it may not be possible and, even if it were, it would not be desirable. If you resume working after retirement, you want to do it because you enjoy it, not because you are forced into it by unwise decisions you made prior to retirement.

CHAPTER THREE

It's Not About the Market, It's About the Math

"I never attempt to make money on the stock market. I buy on the assumption that they could close the market the next day and not reopen it for five years."

~ *Warren Buffett*

If you like roller coasters, Knott's Berry Farm, an amusement park located about 30 minutes north of our office in Irvine, California, is your kind of place.

The Silver Bullet is an inversion roller coaster, which simply means the ride is designed to turn you upside down six times as you go around the track at over 50 miles per hour. As roller coasters go, this one is not for the faint of heart. At one point on the two-minute thrill ride, you are lifted 146 feet into the air before plummeting 109 feet.

Then there is the Xcelerator. According to its promotional advertising, this monster allows you to rocket from zero to 82 miles per hour in 2.3 seconds and soar hundreds of feet in the air before hurtling 90 degrees straight down. Riders are advised to "hold tight, and make sure your knuckles are white, because this baby burns rubber across 2,202 feet of cool coral track."

The Knott's Berry people give all of their roller coasters themes. The Xcelerator takes you back in time to the 1950s. GhostRider—which claims to be the longest, tallest and fastest wooden roller coaster on the west coast—gives you the sensation of riding in an old runaway mining car on 4,533 feet of undulating track.

Some have compared the dizzy way roller coasters make you feel to the stock market, with its up-one-minute-and-down-the-next thrills. The analogy is a fitting one. The period that began in 2000 saw the market soar to dizzying heights, then plunge steeply downward virtually overnight. At least with roller coasters, you can see what's ahead of you. What makes the stock market a wild ride is you never know what's going to happen next.

The Emotions of Investing

"Buy low, sell high," is a time-honored axiom that investors have been chanting ever since stock exchanges were created as far back as the 16th century. While it may sound simple, it is not. Why? Because emotions get in the way.

Let's face it, the typical do-it-yourself stock market investor doesn't jump on a stock when it is at its lowest. It is usually when the train has already left the station, so to speak. Let's call our investor Bob. Bob gets a tip from Joe at the office. Or he reads an article in a financial magazine. Or he hears an analyst on one of the financial channels on cable TV. He has his eye on a stock. Bob is hesitant at first. Then, as the share price starts begins to increase and gains momentum, Bob makes his move.

Optimism is high. He is excited about what the future will bring. Every morning, when the market opens, Bob can't resist checking his smartphone to see what the ticker symbol is doing. A week goes by. He is thrilled to see his stock is up two bucks per share!

But, as we all know, the market moves in cycles. Bob's euphoria turns to anxiety one Monday when the market opens lower, and his stock begins to give back some of its gains. Hey, wait a minute! This was not in the plan. At first, there is denial. What if the market crashes and takes his stock down with it? Nahhh! It's only a glitch, he tells himself. Then, chiding himself for being so chicken-hearted, he waits nervously for tomorrow's action.

He watches the clock until the opening bell. The market is down again! And so is his stock! By noon, it has given back all its gains and the share price is lower than it was when he made the buy. Fear and depression set in. Bob wonders, should he get out now and cut his losses, or hold on and wait for the comeback? This is real money he is losing! He holds on until the following morning. If it is still sliding down, he will bail out.

Sure enough, on Wednesday, Wall Street is all doom and gloom. His stock is tanking big time. He panics. He can't press the buttons on his online trading account fast enough to dump the stock. Depressed his investment has lost money, he consoles himself that it could have been worse. The stock goes even lower by the end of the trading day.

Thursday comes. He must check his smartphone to see what the stock he no longer owns is doing now. Oh no! the market is recovering! The stock he just dumped is on its way back up the charts. It has gained back almost all its losses and analysts say it could go even higher! Bob wonders what he should do? Get back in now? The cycle starts all over again.

If there is a secret to successful investing, famed investor Warren Buffett, the "Oracle of Omaha," ought to know it. He put it this way: "We simply attempt to be fearful when others are greedy and to be greedy when others are fearful."

That's good advice, but easier said than done. It is difficult to manifest the just the right emotion what's on the line is hard-earned cash you know you will need down the road.

Why do we tend to buy high and sell low? Because we can't help being emotional. As Pogo, the main character in a well-known comic strip drawn by cartoonist Walt Kelly, said, "We have met the enemy and he is us."

If this has ever happened to you, don't feel like the Lone Ranger. According to the financial services research firm DALBAR, that's how the average investor fares—buying just before the market peaks and selling when the losses are too painful to take. That is why the average investor's returns significantly trail those of the market.

DALBAR did a study in 2011 that found, for a 20-year period ending in December of that year, the S&P 500 Index had a 7.81 return, when the average investor's return was only 3.49 percent. In other words, an index may be up 10 percent, but the average Bob will only have 3 or 4 percent to show for it because of knee-jerk decisions made in the heat of emotion. [15]

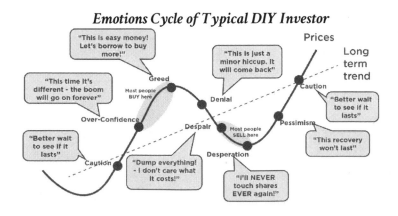

Emotions Cycle of Typical DIY Investor

---

[15] Mandi Woodruff. Business Insider. March 30, 2012. "We Let Emotions Wreck Our Investment Portfolio All Too Easily." www.businessinsider.com/infographic-see-how-easily-we-let-emotions-wreck-our-investment-portfolio-2012-3.

How It All Got Started ✗ *Tulip Story*

Investors riding on their emotions is nothing new. The earliest example of an economic bubble affecting the world's economy is the "tulip bubble" of 1637. As bizarre as it sounds, tulips became a sort of currency when people in the Netherlands began trading them as if they were commodities.

It all started when tulips, which were indigenous to Turkey, were introduced to Europe in the late 1500s. Europeans went crazy over tulips. They thought they were exotically beautiful and found them strangely appealing. Rich people had to have massive tulip gardens of red, yellow and pink gracing their mansions.

Amsterdam merchants, who traded with the East Indies, figured they could make some money selling tulip bulbs, which had become the hottest thing. It was just a fad, but who knew? No one. People were so crazy over tulip bulbs that they were willing to pay exorbitant prices for them. The law of supply and demand was at work.

One factor that added to their demand was the length of time it took for a tulip seed to grow into a bulb—seven to 12 years. Some bulbs were in high demand because they were rare, like the multicolored tulip bulbs.

Along came the speculators. These were people who didn't really want to own tulips; they just wanted to make a quick profit buying and selling the bulbs. Greed took over, and bulb prices started to inflate beyond reason.

As time went on, a "bulb bubble" developed. Traders scrambled to unload their bulbs, but there weren't enough buyers. Panic set in. Prices plummeted. Some unfortunate traders were left holding bulbs they had bought with borrowed money. They lost everything. "Tulip deflation" started in the Netherlands, and soon spread to all of Europe. The great tulip crash of the 1600s affected the economies of all the civilized world in one way or another.[16]

Keeping Your Nest Egg Safe

A point we will make often in this book is this: how you invested when you were 30 is not how you should invest when you are 60. The investing strategies that got you *to* retirement are not the same that will get you *through* retirement.

No one can gaze into a crystal ball and see when the next market crash will occur. The science of standard deviation analysis acknowledges markets are capable of wide swings. Adjusting risk tolerance is essential if we are to successfully maneuver through the investing minefield the stock market has become in the 21st century.

How Would Your Life Change If...

If you were to experience a 50 percent gain in your portfolio, how would it change your life? Would it alter your lifestyle significantly? Most people say no. While they might add a few more comforts here or there, most folks say their lifestyle would remain essentially the same.

But what if you were to *lose* 50 percent of your portfolio? Most people say yes, that would change the way they live considerably. They would start cutting back on unnecessary expenses. They would become more fiscally conservative in every aspect of life.

---

[16] Elena Holodny. Business Insider. Sept. 16, 2014. "How a Country Went Totally Nuts for Flower Bulbs." http://www.businessinsider.com/tulipmania-bubble-story-2014-9.

Losing half of your wealth could even cause worry and stress that would affect your health.

We know of one couple who had to seek marriage counseling to repair their relationship after the 2008 market crash. They were a year away from retiring and lost nearly half their life's savings. Financial windfalls are icing on the cake, but financial setbacks can take a tremendous toll. You just don't want money problems haunting your "golden years."

In the past quarter century, we have met with hundreds of people who are approaching retirement and those already retired. Many of them are professional people—bright and well-educated. But the most common mistake they make is not understanding how much risk they are taking with their investments. Which is why risk analysis is first on the task checklist when we are hired to help them.

During our working years, our most valuable asset is ourselves. We are, after all, producing the income. When we retire, that importance should be transferred to our portfolio, which will be providing us with paychecks. That's why we must learn to treat our portfolio much differently in our retirement than we did in our working years. We want growth, sure. But protecting the assets we have worked so hard to accumulate becomes our priority.

The bottom line is this: your income in retirement shouldn't depend on the markets, it should depend on math. Hopefully you have a strategic income plan that will employ a portion of your assets in the stock market, but allow the majority of your employable wealth to generate (a) income you cannot outlive, and (b) income that increases over time to compensate for inflation. We call such planning S.I.I.P., which stands for Strategic Income and Inheritance Plan. The goal is to lock in retirement income for both spouses if you are married, minimize market risk, and leave a lasting legacy for your loved ones.

Action Plan

Once your income plan is established, you should assess risk tolerance and evaluate ways to reduce risk while still accomplishing your long-range financial goals.

CHAPTER FOUR

Beware of Hidden Fees

"Nothing in fine print is ever good news."
~ Andy Rooney

T he mood was festive aboard the Italian cruise ship on the night of Jan. 13, 2013. Shortly after 9 p.m., many of the 3,229 passengers aboard the vessel were still in the ship's spacious dining room, lingering over their evening meal. The captain had steered a course that would take the ship just off the coast of Giglio, an island that lay a mere 10 miles off the western coast of Italy. He would explain later he wanted to give the island a "sail-by salute." Suddenly, people onboard the Costa Concordia felt a jolt and heard and a low, wrenching sound. The ship had struck an underwater rock formation and the collision had sliced the hull open like a can opener. Water gushed through a 160-foot gash on the ship's port side, flooding the engine room, causing the Costa Concordia to lose power. She drifted to within 500 yards of a small village on the island where she came to rest on her starboard side. In a disastrous evacuation, many passengers jumped overboard to swim to shore, and 32 cruise passengers lost their lives. For months, the 114,000-ton cruise liner lay partially submerged. Salvagers eventually refloated her and sold her for scrap. The ship had cost $612 million to build. The total cost of the disaster, including compensation to victims, refloating, towing and scrapping costs, was approximately $2 billion.[17]

Beware of Hidden Fees

Like those rocks lurking beneath the surface of the water, undetected hidden fees and concealed charges can pose a serious threat to our investment vehicles if we are not vigilant. In the case of the Costa Concordia, the reef was clearly marked on the nautical charts; the captain just steered off course. The unnecessary charges that rob us of returns on our investments are usually concealed in the documents' fine print.

If you detest fine print, you are not alone. It's ubiquitous in everything we buy, from food labels to phone bills. In fact, the smaller the print the more likelihood you are getting ripped off. At least, that's the impression we get.

Banks like to slip in maintenance fees and transaction fees. Phone companies like to charge service fees and surcharges that they figure most people will just shut their eyes and pay. They are right! We do.

Even grocery stores are getting in on the act.

A 2016 article by J.D. Roth entitled "Hidden Price Increases at the Grocery Store," told of shoppers buying the same product they had been using for years, only to discover the container and the contents had shrunk. A yogurt container that once held 8 ounces shrinks a bit and contains 6 ounces for the same price. Fabric softeners cut their sheet count from 40 to 36 for the same price. Ketchup bottles hold less and cost the same. A carton of ice cream

---

[17] The Guardian. "Costa Concordia" https://www.theguardian.com/world/costa-concordia.

that once contained 16 ounces now contains 14 ounces for the same price.

Who do these food producers think they are dealing with? A bunch of naïve shoppers who don't pay attention? Yep. And they're right![18]

The same goes for unwary investors, most of whom pay hidden fees and charges on mutual funds and variable annuities and are blithely unaware.

Danger Zones

Some of the worst offenders in this area are mutual funds. In its issue of March 2, 2013, the highly respected financial magazine *Barron's* ran an article titled, "The Hidden Cost of Doing Business," which cites the research of finance professor Roger Edelen of the University of California. He identifies trading costs, or transaction costs, as the invisible culprits that eat away at mutual fund returns.

Goodman explains: *"Transaction or trading costs include the commissions paid, the bid-ask spread on each transaction, and the price, or*

---

[18] J.D. Roth. Get Rich Slowly. Sept. 19, 2016 "Hidden Price Increases at the Grocery Store." http://www.getrichslowly.org/2008/07/29/hidden-price-increases-at-the-grocery-store/.

market, impact of funds buying or selling big blocks of shares. (When a fund buys or sells a substantial amount of a company's stock, it can "move the market," causing the share price to rise or fall, thereby putting it in the unfortunate position of continuing to buy while the price is rising, or selling as the price is falling.)"

Most investors pay little attention to transaction costs when the funds are performing well. They allow it is just "the cost of doing business." But if the funds start to lose money, these hidden fees show up like sharp rocks at low tide. Goodman estimates the average mutual fund investor pays 1.44 percent annually in transaction costs. Remember, you pay these costs whether or not you receive positive returns!

Commissions are disclosed in the mutual fund's prospectus, true, but Professor Goodman says this can be misleading.

"They can make the stated commissions arbitrarily low," says Goodman, "but Wall Street finds a way to get paid."

People are more likely to read the ingredients on the back of a cereal box than they are to read their mutual fund prospectus. The average investor tunes out just looking at the pages. Ever wonder why the language is difficult to comprehend? Could it be that the fund firms prefer we remain in the dark?[19]

Another article, "The Investment Fees You Don't Realize You're Paying," appeared in the Dec. 15, 2014 issue of *U.S. News and World Report* and quoted a survey by the investment firm Rebalance IRA. The survey revealed many mutual fund investors were surprised to learn they were paying any fees at all. Here's a quote from the article:

"Rebalance IRA asked 1,165 baby boomers between ages 50 and 68, all with full-time jobs, how much they were paying in investment fees. Forty-six percent believed they paid nothing, and 19 percent were under the

---

[19] Beverly Goodman. Barron's. March 2, 2013. "The Hidden Cost of Doing Business."
http://www.barrons.com/articles/SB50001424052748704356104578326293404837234.

impression that their fees totaled less than 0.5 percent. In fact, according to data cited by Rebalance IRA, employees have retirement account expense deductions averaging 1.5 percent per year."

The article's author, Kate Stalter, offers the following suggestions to avoid hidden investment fees:

- Have an investment strategy—instead of just investing for investing's sake, identify your goals and risk tolerance. Once you establish a strategy, stick with it and stay disciplined.

- Consider the type of investment carefully—some accounts are taxable and some are not. Know the difference. A taxable account with a high level of trading will cost you more.

- Know how your financial advisor is paid—is the advisor a traditional broker who is paid a commission every time a trade is made? Or is he or she a Registered Investment Advisor who receives a percentage of assets under management or a flat fee?

- Read and understand your statement—she uses the example of one financial advisor who reportedly broke out the fees on a portfolio quarterly. The investor was paying 0.37 percent *per quarter,* which totals out to 1.5 *per year.* You had to do the math and multiply times four to get the true picture.

- Understand mutual fund fee structures—learn the difference between Class A, B, C, R and I. Some have front-end loads deducted from the initial investment. Look for 12-b1 fees. Those are internal expenses and they are built into most mutual funds. Check out the internal expense ratio.

Naturally, the lower the cost, the more of your returns you get to keep if the fund does well.[20]

To illustrate the extent to which trading (transaction) fees can eat into your investment, assume you have $500,000 in a mutual fund portfolio, and you are paying 2 percent in fees. Two percent of $500,000 is $10,000. That's how much you are paying **per year** for that investment! Has the fund's performance in the last 10 years or so warranted that kind of cash outlay? Probably not, but that is for you to decide. Our point is, most people are unaware of what they are paying. If you think any of this applies to you, get an objective analysis from an unbiased advisor—a second opinion in other words. Also, when you read advertisements from the mutual fund industry about performance, look for information about the costs involved. You may not find much published on this. Remember, high investment costs erode good investment performance.

Brokerage Account Fees

Most people know stockbrokers and brokerage firms charge commissions. They compete with other stockbrokers and brokerage firms and publish comparison tables. If you pick up one of these advertisements, you may find them difficult to decipher. There are lots of asterisks and fine print. As with any advertisement, the company producing the advertisement wants you to think they charge less than the competition. For example, one broker posts $10 per trade while another advertises $17 per trade. Which one do you go with? You assume the $10 per trade is less

---

[20] Kate Stalter. U.S. News & World Report. Dec. 15, 2014. "The Investment Fees You Don't Realize You're Paying." http://money.usnews.com/money/personal-finance/mutual-funds/articles/2014/12/15/the-investment-fees-youre-dont-realize-youre-paying.

Have Team look into Vanguard, Schwab, etc.

expensive, but the fine print may reveal you pay extra if you want to talk to a real, live human being about your investment. You may also learn, as you read on, you are subject to pay an "inactivity fee" if you leave the account idle too long. Some brokerage firms charge you a fee to deposit money into the account.

The ordinary investor will not try to understand these tables. Imagine sitting down at a nice restaurant, opening your menu, and seeing the price of a salad is $5.00. Then, you notice a tiny asterisk beside the price. At the bottom of the menu in small print you read that you pay extra for tomato-slicing and carrot-peeling. Another asterisk informs you there is a delivery fee and the salad dressing is an add-on, making the total cost of the salad over $15.00. Walk out? Yeah, us too.

It's the Principle of the Thing

It's not so much the money as it is the principle of the thing. The Ponemon Institute conducted a study in 2006, which concluded that sneaky charges and hidden fees cost the average American consumer just shy of $1,000 each year. Larry Ponemon, founder of the research group, revisited the figures in 2009 and estimated the "sneaky fees" phenomenon has worsened by some 10-20 percent since the study was conducted.[21]

A Word of Caution from the SEC

The website for the United States Securities and Exchange Commission is www.sec.gov. Under the heading *Calculating Mutual Fund Fees and Expenses,* you will find the following paragraphs:

---

[21] Bob Sullivan. Ballentine Books. Dec. 26, 2007. "Gotcha Capitalism."

*"Fees and expenses are an important consideration in selecting a mutual fund because **these charges lower your returns.** Many investors find it helpful to compare the fees and expenses of different mutual funds before they invest."*

"A mutual fund's fees and expenses may be more important than you realize. Advertisements, rankings and ratings often emphasize how well a fund has performed in the past. But studies show that the future is often different. This year's 'number one' fund can easily become next year's below average fund." [22]

The personal finance website NerdWallet.com warns: "investment expenses directly reduce your portfolio's return. If your portfolio was up 6 percent for the year but you paid 1.5 percent in fees and expenses, your return is actually only 4.5 percent. Over time, that difference really adds up."

Transparency in Statements

A 72-year-old retired college professor came into our office in Irvine, California, one day for a consultation. She was frustrated with her brokerage statement.

"I'm an educated woman, but I can't understand this thing," she said, holding up a copy of her brokerage statement.

The woman said she had lost around 40 percent of her portfolio during the 2008 market crash. She said she had informed her broker prior to the financial crisis that she wanted to be conservative in her investments, and the broker's response to her was that she was "very well diversified," and was therefore at minimum risk.

---

[22] U.S. Securities and Exchange Commission. Aug. 10, 2010. "Calculating Mutual Fund Fees and Expenses." https://www.sec.gov/reportspubs/investor-publications/investortoolsmfccmfcc-inthtm.html.

Her statement revealed her assets were 85 percent at risk—highly inappropriate for an investor of her age. Why? Had the broker disregarded her requests to be conservative? Or did the broker not have the tools to put her into low-risk investments?

We did a line-by-line explanation of her statement and found something even more troubling. Each month during her account's decline, she had paid handsomely in transaction fees and other charges for the privilege of losing money.

Hidden 401(k) Fees

On July 1, 2012, a new law went into effect requiring 401(k) plan administrators to give employees full details of fees they are paying. A study conducted by AARP asked employees of large corporations if they thought they were paying fees when they made contributions to their 401(k)s. Seventy-one percent said no. Many were surprised to learn they paid for fees for record-keeping, administrative fees and various other charges.

"What You're About to Learn Will Shock You" is the title of a June 25, 2012, article written by Ross Kenneth Urken of *AOL Daily Finance*. Urken interviewed Robyn Credico, senior consultant at Towers Watson, a New York-based human resources consulting firm. "Sometimes those investment companies say to the record keeper, 'I'll give you a little bit of the investment to offset your record-keeping fees,' "Credico said.[23]

In plain language, we call that (allowing third-party managers to receive revenue sharing from mutual fund companies) a *kickback*. In other words, a TPA (third-party administrator), or brokerage house, that manages a mutual fund receives an under-the-

---

[23] Ross Kenneth Urken. AOL.com. June 25, 2012. "401(k) Fees: What You're About to Learn Will Shock You." https://www.aol.com/2012/06/25/401k-fees-disclosure-rules-action/.

table cut of your investment and pays the record keeper. Under new rules, the U.S. Department of Labor will require 401(k) plan administrators to reveal to employers how much they (employees) are paying in fees for every $1,000 invested.[24]

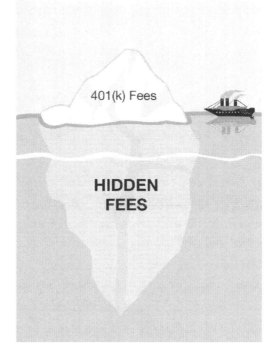

In another *Daily Finance* article, "Hidden 401(k) Fees: The Great Retirement Plan Rip-Off," Adam J. Wiederman said, "The typical 401(k) will steal an average of nearly $155,000 from each worker over a lifetime of saving. The reason for this massive loss of wealth over a lifetime of saving comes down to fees. Those fees are usually expressed in a way that disguises the true cost."

According to Wiederman, "Trading fees are costs incurred when a mutual fund buys or sells an investment, in the form of

---

[24] Ibid.

commissions and bid/ask spreads (the difference between the price the fund actually buys or sells an asset for versus its market value). They vary based on how actively a mutual fund is trading." Then he adds, "But good luck trying to figure out how much you're actually paying for trading fees."[25]

Mutual Fund Hidden Costs

According to a *Wall Street Journal* article, "The Hidden Cost of Mutual Funds," expense ratios of a mutual fund are not the real bottom line. Other unreported costs are the real bottom line. "There are other costs, not reported in the expense ratio, related to the buying and selling of securities in the portfolio, and those expenses can make a fund two or three times as costly as advertised," writes Anna Prior.[26]

An extra percent or two in fees and charges per year can make a big difference to a retiree's lifestyle. We know one couple who love visiting national parks in their small motor home. They take full advantage of the "senior pass" program, which, for a nominal application fee, allows permanent U.S. residents over age 62 to visit over 2,000 recreation areas across the nation at little or no cost. They enjoy their freedom in retirement, and they have $500,000 portfolio. But they do not consider themselves wealthy. They say they must watch their expenses to maintain the lifestyle they both love.

When you convert percentages to dollars, if they are paying fees of 2-3 percent on their portfolio of half a million dollars, that's $20,000 to $30,000 a year. If they could cut those fees in half,

---

[25] Ibid.

[26] Anna Prior. Wall Street Journal. March 1, 2010. "The Hidden Cost of Mutual Funds."
https://www.wsj.com/articles/SB10001424052748703382904575059690954870722.

it would give them an extra $10,000 to $15,000 in traveling money each year. That could mean a lot to this couple. One of their passions in life—aside from taking in the beauty of America—is to help provide a good education for their two grandsons. That kind of money could go a long way toward accomplishing that goal. Plowing that money back into their investments could have a cumulative effect on their returns.

If $10,000 or $15,000 were falling through the cracks in your investment account, when would you want to know about it? Right away? Yeah, we would too.

John "Jack" Bogle, founder of The Vanguard Group, says "Costs are a crucial part of the [investing] equation." In an April 2013 *Frontline/PBS* documentary, Bogle quipped, "It doesn't take a genius to know that the bigger the profit of the management company, the smaller the profit investors get. The money managers always want more, and that seems natural for most businesses, but it's not right for this business."

Bogle pointed out that, over a 50-year period, even seemingly small fees can compound to take a third or more of your portfolio. "What happens in the fund business is that magic of compound returns is overwhelmed by the tyranny of compounding costs," he said. "It's a mathematical fact. There's no getting around it. But the fact that we don't look at it (is) too bad for us... If you want to gamble with your retirement money, all I can say is 'be my guest.' But be aware of the mathematical reality... It has been proven right year after year after year. It can't be proven wrong. It's a mathematical certainty."

Bogle continued, "Do you want to invest in a system where you put up 100 percent of the capital, where you take 100 percent of the risk, and you get 30 percent of the return?"[27]

Ron Lieber, who writes the "Your Money" column for *The New York Times*, is another critic of hidden investment fees.

"The fees may not seem like much," Lieber explained. "You've got $50,000 or $100,000 in your portfolio, and you might lose $500 or $1,000 year. That's what you would pay to a financial advisor, right? But, if you add that up over 20 or 30 or even 50 years, you're well into six figures as your balance grows. That's the difference between running out of money before you die, and having a little money left to pass on to your heirs."[28, 29]

Action Plan

Adjust your portfolio to reduce or eliminate fees.

---

[27] Jason Breslow with John Bogle. PBS Frontline. April 23, 2013. "The Train Wreck Awaiting American Retirement." http://www.pbs.org/wgbh/frontline/article/john-bogle-the-train-wreck-awaiting-american-retirement/.

[28] Ron Lieber. New York Times. June 10, 2011. "Revealing Hidden Costs of Your 401(k)." http://www.nytimes.com/2011/06/11/your-money/401ks-and-similar-plans/11money.html.

[29] Ron Lieber. New York Times. Jan. 1, 2010. "For Savers, It Was Hardly a Lost Decade." http://www.nytimes.com/2010/01/02/your-money/stocks-and-bonds/02money.html.

CHAPTER FIVE

What About Taxes

"The nine most terrifying words in the English language are: I'm from the government and I'm here to help."
~ *Ronald Reagan*

We think one of the biggest traps people fall into when they are planning for retirement is underestimating the tax monster and the bite he can take out of their savings.

If you are like most folks, when you retire, you will be withdrawing your money from your savings and investments to replace the paycheck you were receiving when you were working. Well, how you make that withdrawal makes a lot of difference.

Commonly held wisdom says it is best to use money from taxable accounts first and then tap your tax-deferred retirement accounts—IRAs and 401(k)s, etc. Next, the thinking goes, tap into your accounts where taxes have already been paid, like Roth accounts.

That works for many retirees. But, a word of caution. What if most of your savings is in your 401(k) or a traditional IRA and you hit the RMD (required minimum distribution) zone—when you turn 70 ½. Those RMDs, depending on how large those accounts are, could put you into a higher tax bracket. If that is the case, you may want to consider moving that money into a more tax favored, RMD-friendly account, or make tax-deferred accounts the first ones you tap.

How is retirement income taxed? It depends on the source. For example: withdrawals from tax-deferred accounts such as 401(k)s and traditional IRAs are taxed as ordinary income, as is interest on CDs, savings accounts and money market accounts.

Interest received from municipal bond is exempt from federal income tax, but you must remember municipal bonds are state-sensitive when it comes to state and local taxes.

Profits you receive when you sell stocks, bonds or mutual funds are taxed as capital gains. Those rates can vary based on the date you purchased the investment and how long you have owned it. Assets held a year or more are taxed at long-term capital gains rates, which are more favorable than short-term capital gains, which are taxed as ordinary income at your current income tax rate.

Got a Roth IRA? If you are older than 59 ½ and have had the account for five years or more, then pat yourself on the back and smile. If you've ever played Monopoly, it's like getting a get-out-of-jail-free card from the tax man. You don't have to take RMDs when you turn 70 ½, either.

What about payment from pensions? Not all pensions are created equal but, typically, pension payments are taxed as ordinary income. An exception is if you made after-tax contributions to the plan

What about annuities? Many people use annuities as a source of income in retirement. First, a disclaimer: there are many types of annuities, and the rules vary widely depending on which type of annuity you own and the source of the purchase funds. Typically, the portion of the annuity payment that represents principal is tax-free and the rest is taxed as ordinary income.

What about Social Security benefits? We talk to many retirees who are shocked to learn their Social Security benefits are subject to taxes. That's the bad news. The good news is—please stay tuned—there may be ways to avoid that.

We are not attempting here to produce a guide to every possible scenario here. That requires a deeper drill. We are merely pointing out that how you structure your income in retirement can affect how much money you pay to Uncle Sam. In most cases, with just a little planning, you can ease your tax burden considerably.

Tax Reduction

Question: What's the difference between tax *evasion* and tax *avoidance?*

Answer: Around 10 to 20 years.

Tax evasion, after all, is a criminal offense. Tax avoidance, however, is entirely legal and ethical. There is nothing unpatriotic, unethical, immoral or illegal about avoiding the overpayment of taxes. Most of us good, red-blooded American citizens want to pay

our fair share of taxes; we just don't like the idea of paying someone else's taxes, or paying a penny more than we rightfully owe.

The rules on paying taxes are published in the Internal Revenue Service Tax Code—a document that has, according to some
sources, more than 4 million words, and 74,608 pages.

To put that in perspective, think of a hard-to-read book with
many pages. Leo Tolstoy's *War and Peace,* for example, has
587,287 words and more than 1,200 pages. All of J.K. Rowling's
Harry Potter books put together have a little over a million words
and 3,791 pages. The Authorized King James Bible contains
783,137 words and, using a standard font, the average bible is
around 1,200 pages long.

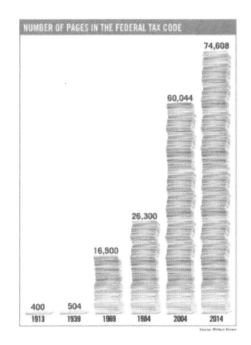

Even the IRS itself admits its tax code is hard to figure out. In
2008, when the IRS published the Taxpayer Advocate Service's
2008 Annual Report to Congress, an excerpt read: "The most seri-

ous problem facing taxpayers is the complexity of the Internal Revenue Code."

Buried in all those millions of words in the IRS code are thousands of ways to avoid unnecessary taxes. Don't bother looking for them under a big, bold heading such as *Tax Breaks*, or *Read This to Avoid Unnecessary Taxation*. It's a treasure hunt and you need a map. If you don't know where to look, you won't find them. In short, you need professional help.[30, 31, 32]

A World of Difference

There is a world of difference between a tax *preparer* and a tax *advisor*. A tax advisor will likely educate you on ways to lower your tax obligation, and not just by telling you to change your withholdings or make bigger contributions to your qualified retirement accounts. You know how to do that on your own. A tax advisor takes the time to go over your entire tax landscape and analyze where you are paying more than you have to. A tax advisor will spot areas where you can save money on taxes both now and in the future. The tax advisor knows where to look in the voluminous IRS code for the provisions that legally enable these savings. Tax preparers render many valuable services, and most certainly know their way around the blanks on a 1040 form, but it seldom goes beyond that. If your return is simple and you want it

[30] Kelly Phillips Erb. Forbes. Jan. 10, 2013. "Tax Code Hits Nearly 4 Million Words." https://www.forbes.com/sites/kellyphillipserb/2013/01/10/tax-code-hits-nearly-4-million-words-taxpayer-advocate-calls-it-too-complicated/#18a7ceab6e24.

[31] Michelle Ye Hee Lee. Washington Post. March 11, 2015. "Ted Cruz's claim that the IRS tax code has more words than the Bible." https://www.washingtonpost.com/news/fact-checker/wp/2015/03/11/ted-cruzs-claim-that-the-irs-tax-code-has-more-words-than-the-bible/?utm_term=.2e796bea868a.

[32] Taxpayer Advocate Service. 2008. "Most Serious Problems: #1 The Complexity of the Tax Code." http://www.irs.gov/pub/tas/08_tas_arc_msp_1.pdf.

prepared quickly, then a tax preparer is just the ticket. But if you want efficiency and direction on how to prevent unnecessary taxation, then you need to consult with a tax advisor.

Tax advisors are also available all year, not just at tax time. They make it their business to keep up with the ever-changing rules and laws of taxes.

Minimizing Taxes on Social Security

The story goes that when President Franklin D. Roosevelt signed the Social Security Act into law in 1935, someone asked him the government would tax Social Security benefits. He responded by pounding on the oval office desk and vowing that he would **never** tax Social Security benefits. After all, what sense would it make to tax benefits going out when taxes were paid on the contributions going into the fund?

If the story is true (the Social Security Administration says it is fiction), you have to hand it to FDR. He kept his promise. As long as he was alive, no taxes were imposed on Social Security benefits. In fact, they remained untaxed until Ronald Reagan was president signed into law the Social Security Amendments of 1983. In 1984, it became law that if your base income as a single taxpayer was $25,000, or if you earned more than $32,000 per year as a married couple filing jointly, then up to 50 percent of your Social Security could be taxed by the Internal Revenue System.[33]

Taxes on Social Security increased under President William Jefferson "Bill" Clinton in 1993. That year, single filers with incomes of more than $34,000 and couples with annual incomes of $44,000 would pay taxes on up to 85 percent of their benefits.

---

[33] Social Security Administration. "Debunking Some Internet Myths." www.ssa.gov/history/InternetMyths.html.

Some retirees are still surprised to learn that Social Security benefits can be taxed.

Social Security Taxation		
Filing Status	*Provisional Income*	*SS Amount Subject to Tax*
Married filing jointly	Under $32,000	0%
	$32,000 - $44,000	50%
	Over $44,000	85%
Single, head of household, qualifying widow(er), married filing separately & living apart from spouse	Under $25,000	0%
	$25,000 - $34,000	50%
	Over $34,000	85%
Married filing separately and living with spouse	Over 0	85%

Keep in mind, how much of your Social Security income is taxable depends on how much of your income is considered taxable by the IRS. Strategies are available that can limit, and in some cases even eliminate, Social Security taxes. It all depends on how much other income you have, and which category it falls into—taxable or non-taxable.

Provisional income is a term used by the IRS to calculate taxes. They calculate it by adding up:

(a) your total gross income (not including Social Security—which you can easily find on your tax return);

(b) any tax-free interest you received—interest on a municipal bond, for example, which is exempt from federal tax;

(c) half of your Social Security benefit.

So, suppose your gross income is $30,000, which you received from returns on investments. Then you earn another $2,000 in municipal bond interest. And let's say your yearly Social Security benefit is $24,000. Then your *provisional income* is $44,000.

So, how can you minimize taxes on Social Security? By lowering your income. But wait a minute! I don't want to *lower my income* just to *lower taxes*! Of course, you don't! But what if you could adjust how your income is *calculated* so you lowered your *reportable* income?

Do you mean to say that certain income is considered reportable by the IRS and other income is not? Absolutely! Stock market gains, for example, are reportable as provisional income, but gains from tax-deferred accounts, such as annuity balances, are not. That's what tax-deferred means! Gains from an annuity will be taxed eventually, but only when you withdraw them. Who is in control of that? You are! Gains on a CD or stock market investment account must be taken each year and reported. Even if you reinvest the money back into the investment account? Yes.

So, one way to maximize income and minimize taxes is to move money from a non-tax-favored category to one that is tax-favored, where gains are not considered to be income by the IRS and are therefore not reportable.

Some of the numbers and other particulars of this discussion are, of course, subject to change. In fact, we may have the table flipped on some of this depending on what the current Congressional session comes up with in their tax plan. This is just one more reason it's a good idea to consult with a fully trained, competent tax advisor who is up-to-date on all the most recent laws and regulations before you make any significant changes.

Synchronizing Retirement Income

Think of your retirement income picture as a machine with several moving parts. For this machine to run smoothly, all the parts must work together. In a word, it must be synchronized.

One cog in this machinery is Social Security. Other moving parts may be pensions (for the fortunate few who have them), IRAs, 401(k)s, income from investments and RMDs from qualified accounts. Also, some we know plan to continue working in retirement, not necessarily because they have to; some just love what they do and want to continue doing it. Others plan to turn their hobbies into a business. If that is the case, then there is also that income to consider. The point is, it's crucial to make those income sources flow harmoniously to avoid tax disadvantages and lost income.

If you wish to convert your nest egg into a life-long income stream, planning is essential. You will need a firm that specializes in retirement income planning and you want professionals who know their way around the tax code and can steer you in the direction that minimizes taxation and maximizes income.

To Roth or Not to Roth?

When Delaware Senator William Roth died in 2003, he left quite a legacy—the eponymous Roth IRA, a plan for tax-free compounded savings that bears his name. The signature benefit of the Roth IRA, introduced in 1997, and the Roth 401(k), introduced in 2006, is that you pay taxes going in, but pay no tax on gains or withdrawals, ever.

The decision between the traditional IRA and the Roth is simple: Do you want your tax break now or when you retire?

Another benefit is you are insulated from income tax rate hikes. Will you be in a higher tax bracket when you retire? Will tax rates be higher in the future? If so, then it makes sense to invest through a Roth and pay Uncle Sam now.

When comparing tax-deferred savings plans with tax-upfront plans, think of a farmer who goes into a feed store to buy seed for spring planting. As he goes to pay for the seed, a man dressed like Uncle Sam leans toward him and says, "Look, I'll make you a deal. You can pay taxes on the seed now and be done with it, or pay no taxes now on the seed but pay me taxes on the harvest."

How long would you have to think before opting to pay Uncle Sam taxes on the seed and not the harvest? That is essentially the choice.

Roth Advantages

Roth IRAs and 401(k)s have no required minimum distributions when you turn 70 ½. You can contribute to a Roth IRA as long as you earn income. There are no age limits, young or old. Since you aren't forced to take money out of a Roth if you don't need it, you can leave it there and let it grow, compounded, tax-free. Over time, that can add up to a considerable sum! Use the money if you need it but, if you don't, leave it to your heirs tax-free. Suppose you retire at age 70 with a $500,000 Roth IRA, but you have other investments and don't need the money. If you leave it alone and let it grow at, say, 6 percent per year, your account could grow to as much as $1.2 million by the time you turn 85. If you leave it to heirs, they won't be able to let the inherited Roth compound tax-free indefinitely. They will be subject to minimum distributions based on their age in the year following your death.

Unlike the original account holder, the inheritor cannot let money in an inherited Roth IRA compound tax-free indefinitely.

The Motley Fool, a web-based investment advice group, says the Roth can be a "retirement plan and an emergency fund in one," since you can withdraw your contributions (not your gains) at any time for any reason. In other words, if you have contributed $5,000 to a Roth IRA for 20 years, then you can access $100,000 whenever you want. If you want to access your investment gains early without penalty, you must have a reason, such as buying your first home, or covering certain education expenses.[34]

Are we fans of Roth IRAs? Yes, in general. But they don't fit into everyone's retirement picture. If you have an existing IRA, should you convert to a Roth? That is a good question, and one that cannot be answered without due diligence. Your unique and individual financial situation must be considered. There are many possible advantages and disadvantages. The job of a competent retirement advisory team is to present the facts, educate you on your options, and help you research the decisions carefully before making one. Buying a life insurance policy may be a better way to leave tax-free money to heirs. That will also depend on your individual situation. There's more than one way to skin a cat, crack an egg and … avoid paying unnecessary taxes when you retire.

---

[34] Matthew Frankel. The Motley Fool. Aug. 4, 2015. "The 4 Best Roth IRA Benefits." www.fool.com/retirement/iras/2015/08/04/the-4-best-roth-ira-benefits.

CHAPTER SIX

Getting the Most
From Social Security

"A Nation's strength lies in the well-being of its people. The Social Security program plays an important part in providing for families, children and older persons in time of stress, but it cannot remain static. Changes in our population, in our working habits, and in our standard of living require constant revision."

> *~ President John Fitzgerald Kennedy*
> *June 30, 1961*

Say what you will about the inadequacies of Social Security to fund the lifestyle of the average American in retirement, it still has some unique advantages. For one thing, you stand to receive a check every month for the rest of your life, no matter how long you live, and regardless of what the economy does or doesn't do. That's something. Your benefits are adjusted upward for inflation. That's good. Of all the folks we know who point out their Social Security benefits represent only a small portion of what they need to comfortably retire, we know of none who have refused to take them. So, it's to our advantage to learn as much as we can about how to get the most from the program.

The rules the government uses to calculate Social Security earnings are complex. That should come as no surprise to us. Anything designed and administered by the government seems to be inherently complex. We have to say, however, the Social Security Administration's website (www.ssa.gov) goes out of its way to explain those rules in plain language.

It Pays to Wait

If you haven't gone to the website and opened up your *"My Social Security"* account, we encourage you to do so. Once you enter your information and establish your password, you will be able to print your Social Security statement. These statements used to appear in your mailbox every year, but budget cutbacks forced the SSA to discontinue sending them in 2011. These documents are useful for retirement income planning. You will see your earnings history since you began working and a calculation of your projected benefits at various retirement ages. A full and very clear explanation is given of how Uncle Sam calculates your Social Security benefits.

One of the most revealing sections of the document tells you how much you will receive if you collect your Social Security benefits (a) as soon as you are eligible (age 62 for most folks), and (b) what they will be if you wait until you are 70.

Yes, you can collect Social Security retirement benefits as early as age 62. But do you want to? It pays to wait until you are age 70 if you can afford to. Why? Because your benefits will increase at the rate of approximately 8 percent (plus inflation) each year you delay. That is not a bad rate of return for an account bearing no risk. For people who were born between 1943 and 1954, full retirement age is 66 (age 67 for those born after 1960). It makes no sense to wait after you turn 70, because your benefits remain static after that.

There are exceptions. Forget everything we said about waiting if you (a) are terminally ill or (b) if you need the cash. But if those two things don't apply, it usually pays to wait.

Loophole Closed

CNN Money put together an interesting piece in March 2015 called "7 Ways to Maximize Your Social Security Benefits," in which writer Jeanne Sahadi pointed out that there are more than 2,700 rules governing Social Security payouts, and if you make the wrong decision, "you could leave tens of thousands of dollars on the table." The CNN piece cites the work of economist Laurence Kotlikoff and financial journalists Philip Moeller and Paul Solman, who coauthored the book, *Get What's Yours: The Secrets to Maxing Out Your Social Security.* Both the CNN article and the Moeller/Solman book are good resources, but you want to be careful when it comes advice on this topic. The Bipartisan Budget Act, which became law Nov. 2, 2015, made some changes to Social Security's laws about claiming *spousal benefits.* The law closed what the Social Security Administration admitted were "unintended loopholes" used by married couples to milk more out of Social Security than the program originally intended.

The loophole allowed some married couples 66 or older who were dual earners to start receiving spousal payments worth half of the higher earner's benefit amount, and then later switch to payments based on their own work record, which would then be higher due to delayed claiming. It was good while it lasted, but now, people who turn 62 on Jan. 2, 2016, or later will no longer be able to claim both a spousal payment and an individual payment at different times. Now you may only receive the higher of the two benefits.[35]

Social Security in Trouble?

If you download your personal Social Security statement and read through it, you will notice the latest versions of this document do not include on Page One the two scary paragraphs we mentioned in Chapter One of this book about the endangered Social Security "facing serious financial problems." Gone is the warning that "action is needed soon to make sure the system will be sound when today's younger workers are ready for retirement." The government offers no explanation for removing the paragraph. Perhaps it is because changes are in the works that will fix the problem. Baby boomers can take heart that the system's problems would not affect them, anyway. For the children of boomers, however, that's another matter. The SSA warned that "without changes, by 2041, the Social Security Trust Fund will be exhausted and there will be enough only pay 75 for each dollar of scheduled benefits."

The nickname sociologists give to the children of baby boomers is "Generation X." To be a Gen-Xer you have to have been born after 1964. Douglas Coupland, who wrote the book *Generation X,* was interviewed in 1991 by *The Harvard Crimson,* student newspaper of Harvard University. When asked what the average American born after 1964 thought about Social Security, he said their outlook was dismal. "They will probably say something like, 'I'll never see any of it. When I get those statements in the mail, I just throw them away.'"

---

[35] Emily Brandon. U.S. News & World Report. Oct. 18, 2010. "6 Social Security Changes Coming in 2017." https://money.usnews.com/money/blogs/planning-to-retire/articles/2016-10-18/6-social-security-changes-coming-in-2017.

Keep in mind, Gen-Xers, those doom-and-gloom projections assume that (a) you will retire at 65, and (b) nothing will be done to fix the system. As we write this, changes are already "in the works" to raise the full retirement age. It may be age 68 by the time you retire, according to AARP. But that won't kill you. You should be living longer than your parents, anyway, if the current trend holds true. There is also talk of increasing the Payroll Tax Cap and recalculating the cost-of-living adjustments. Those and other solutions should "fix" the projected shortfall and extend the viability of Social Security well into the 21st century.[36, 37]

In the 2017 version of the Social Security statement, the SSA acknowledges that Social Security benefits "are not intended to be your only source of income when you retire. On average, Social Security will replace about 40 percent of your annual pre-retirement earnings. You will need other savings, investments, pensions or retirement accounts to live comfortably when you retire."

What a classic understatement!

According to *The Motley Fool* financial writer Todd Campbell, in 2017, if you claim your benefits at "full retirement age" of 66, the maximum monthly benefit you could receive from Social Security would be $2,687 per month. By waiting until age 70, the most you could possibly receive would be $3,538 in 2017.[38]

So, how much income do you need to retire comfortably? That's a loaded question. The obvious answer is *it depends on your*

---

[36] AARP. October 2015. "Updating Social Security for the 21st Century: 12 Proposals You Should Know About." www.aarp.org/work/social-security/info-05-2012/future-of-social-security-proposals.

[37] Ruth Davis Konigsberg. Time. August 3, 2014. "Why Millennials and Gen Xers Shouldn't Diss Social Security." www.time.com/money/3077952/social-security-millennial-gen-x-can-still-count-on-it/.

[38] Todd Campbell. The Motley Fool. "What's the Maximum Social Security Benefit in 2017?" https://www.fool.com/retirement/2016/11/06/whats-the-maximum-social-security-benefit-in-2017.aspx.

lifestyle. Carolyn O'Hara, financial writer for AARP, the magazine, made the following observation in 2015:

"There is no way of knowing what will happen to interest rates and inflation in future years. But for a retiree to generate $40,000 a year after stopping work, he or she will need savings of about $1.18 million to support a 30-year retirement; this was calculated using average returns of 6 percent and inflation at 2.5 percent, according to Morningstar, a Chicago-based investment research firm."

O'Hara acknowledges that each person, each couple, must determine that for themselves, taking into consideration what living costs will be and whether your savings will generate enough cash.

But it is abundantly clear that Social Security, while it will help, will not be enough for the vast majority of retirees in the 21st century.[39]

---

[39] Carolyn O'Hara. AARP. 2015. "How Much Money Do I Need to Retire?" www.aarp.org/work/retirement-planning/info-2015/nest-egg-retirement-amount.

CHAPTER SEVEN

Health Care—the Elephant in the Room

"It is health that is real wealth—not pieces of gold or silver."
~ *Mahatma Ghandi*

It was hot and dry in the late summer/early fall of 2016 in Southern California—just the right conditions for forest fires. Fire crews numbering in the thousands were battling blazes that would ultimately destroy thousands of acres of pristine forest land and turn expensive homes into smoldering cinders.

On Aug. 16, 2016, the Blue Cut fire raged near the Sheep Mountain Wilderness in the San Gabriel Mountains, just 50 miles or so northeast of Irvine, California, where we work and live. That fire destroyed 105 homes and forced 80,000 people to evacuate. It was heart-wrenching to see on the evening news people returning to smoking ruins and weeping over what had once been their spacious and beautiful houses.[40]

---

[40] Sara Parvini, Ruben Vives and Frank Shyong. LA Times. Aug. 20, 2016. "Blue Cut fire in the Cajon Pass destroys 105 homes and 213 other buildings." http://www.latimes.com/local/lanow/la-me-ln-blue-cut-fire-20160819-snap-story.html.

According to the California Department of Forestry and Fire Protection, the Blue Cut fire was only one of 5,762 wildfires that would afflict bone-dry California during the 2016 fire season, burning 147,373 acres and destroying thousands of homes.[41] This was, of course, followed up by 2017's own blazing devastation.

When you began to calculate the financial ramifications of million-dollar homes gone up in smoke, you might have drawn the conclusion that now fire insurance would be either impossible to obtain, or at the least prohibitively costly. But you would be wrong. As we write this book, homeowners' insurance premiums are holding steady in California, according to ValuePenguin.com, a website that tracks such things. They say the average cost of California homeowner's insurance in 2017 was just under $1,000 per year. That's almost half the cost of insuring a home in Florida.[42]

As a last resort, California homeowners who can't find an insurer can turn to a program mandated by the state called FAIR, which stands for Fair Access to Insurance Requirements. The bottom line is, protection is available, and usually at a reasonable cost.

But that's the way insurance is supposed to work, isn't it? Spreading the risk should make it affordable for the masses. The premiums paid by the millions of homeowners whose homes were not touched by the fires keeps the insurance affordable for those whose homes were in the danger zone.

Insurance premiums are calculated by actuaries. It is the job of these professional number-crunchers to calculate the odds of (fill in the blank here with whatever you are trying to protect yourself from) happening to you. That's why car insurance is costlier for younger drivers. Their inexperience and presumed lack of judge-

---

[41] California.gov. 2017. "Incident Information: Number of Fires and Acres." http://cdfdata.fire.ca.gov/incidents/incidents_stats?year=2016.

[42] Value Penguin. 2017. "Average Cost of Homeowners Insurance (2017)." https://www.valuepenguin.com/average-cost-of-homeowners-insurance.

ment behind the wheel means, statistically, chances of them having an accident are greater.

With that in mind, now focus on the elephant in the room: the chances of your needing some form of long-term care in your sunset years. In the case of fire insurance and automobile insurance, the odds are in your favor that you will pay for the insurance and never need it. In the case of long-term care insurance, the odds are that you will.

The Chances of Long-Term Care

Long-term care is a sticky subject. Most people would rather not talk about it and pretend it isn't there. Call it human nature. After all, no one wants to dwell on the unsettling thought of losing one's independence. The idea of living in a long-term health care facility, or, even worse, becoming a burden on their families or a ward of the state, is not something anyone wants to imagine.

NOBODY WANTS TO NOTICE I'M HERE

What are the chances of needing long-term care in one's life? Well, if you live long enough, they are pretty high.

Wade Pfau is a Professor of Retirement Income at The American College in Bryn Mawr, Pennsylvania. He wrote an article that appeared in Forbes magazine on Jan. 5, 2016, in which he points out that 58 percent of men and 79 percent of women aged 65 and older will need long-term care at some point in their lives. He also found research that projects the average lengths for care at 2.2 years for men and 3.7 years for women.[43]

In the article, Pfau acknowledges that statistics vary on this projection, but not much. The Center for Retirement Research at Boston College, for example, estimates 44 percent of men and 58 percent of women will specifically need nursing home care at or after age 65. Pfau writes, "The more general point for this discussion is that many retirees will require long-term care support during their lifetimes, and that the probabilities that this will happen are large enough to warrant some careful planning."[44]

Projected Long-Term Care Needs for 65-Year-Olds in 2005

	Men	Women	All
Percentage who will need care	58%	79%	69%
Average number of years	2.2	3.7	3
Percentage needing no care	42%	21%	31%
Percentage needing 1 year or less	19%	16%	17%
Percentage needing 1-2 years	10%	13%	12%
Percentage needing 2-5 years	17%	22%	20%
Percentage needing 5+ years	11%	28%	20%
Source: Kemper, Komisar and Alecxih (2005)			

---

[43] Wade Pfau. Forbes. Jan. 5, 2016. "Costs and Incidence of Long-Term Care." https://www.forbes.com/sites/wadepfau/2016/01/05/costs-and-incidence-of-long-term-care/#2f6671b64ceb.

[44] Ibid.

What usually triggers long-term care? It is usually a chronic illness, or a condition such as Alzheimer's disease, or an event, such as an accident or a stroke. Ironically, people blessed with longevity in their families are at the same time vulnerable to the curse of mental decline in their later years. So, any way you look at it, it's not a pretty picture.

The Costs of Long-Term Care

How much you will pay for long-term care will depend on (a) where you live, (b) how long you will require the care, and (c) the level of care received. Pfau cites the annual Cost of Care Survey by Genworth, a major provider of long-term care insurance, as one of the best resources to help sort this out.

As of 2016, Genworth puts the median annual cost of a semi-private nursing home room at $91,250. That means a five-year stay in a nursing home would cost $456,250. Pfau points out, "Someone afflicted with Alzheimer's might require care for 10 years or more," at a cost of more than $1 million.

Genworth puts the annual cost of a semi-private room in a nursing home in Orange County, California, at $92,809 per year as of 2016, with a five-year annual growth rate of 2 percent. A private room will cost an average of $146,650 with a five-year annual growth rate of 8 percent. The average cost of other services in Orange County are listed as:

- Home Health Care - $48,000
- Adult Day Health Care - $20,865
- Assisted Living Facility - $48,000

Keep in mind these are averages. Individual costs can vary greatly. Pfau points out that, within the continental United States, "Connecticut is most expensive with a $158,775 median annual cost. The cheapest state is Oklahoma, where the annual median cost is $60,225."

Did you notice that these costs are rising? According to Pfau's research, long-term-care costs are rising faster than overall consumer price inflation. Why is that? In recent years, more people are needing care than the number of facilities providing it. We can't imagine that situation improving in the foreseeable future, considering the stampede of retiring baby boomers approaching their 70s and 80s.

Cost of LTC Insurance

Unless you have millions of disposable cash in reserve, the first thought that comes to mind is insurance. But to quote the words of Commander James Lovell made popular by the movie *Apollo 13,* when the command module exploded, "Uh, Houston... we have a problem."

As we said earlier, what makes the concept of insurance viable, and what makes insurance affordable, is (a) the element of unpredictability, and (b) spreading the risk. For example, actuaries can calculate the average human lifespan. That's what makes the cost of life insurance calculable and affordable. Those wildfires mentioned earlier in this chapter, cataclysmic as they were to those who lost their homes, did not substantially affect the affordability of fire insurance. According to the National Fire Protection Association, the odds of your house burning down are roughly three out of 100. But the odds of your eventually needing long-term care are pretty high. According to the U.S. Department of Health and Human Services, 70 percent of people turning 65 can expect to use some form of long-term care during their lives. Think about that in comparison to the chances of other financial catastrophes. We can easily see why long-term-care insurance is a costly proposition and why, according to the National Bureau of Economic Research, only 10 percent of the elderly have a private long-term care insurance plan.[45, 46]

The way traditional long-term-care insurance works—or any insurance for that matter—the insurance company is betting you won't need it, and you are betting you will. Insurance companies are in business to make a profit. Before they sell you long-term-care insurance that will pay for a nursing home, assisted living or home health care, they will try to ascertain your likelihood of needing the care. Naturally, they will be interested in your age. Younger people are less likely to need the care. They will want to know about your health. If you are ill, you will likely not qualify. The younger you are, and the healthier you are, the easier you will qualify and the lower your premiums will be.

But a word of caution here. How do you know your premiums will remain the same? You don't. There are no guarantees of that with traditional long-term-care insurance. How do you know the costs of long-term care will not increase? You don't. In fact, there is a great likelihood they will. Also, traditional long-term-care insurance is a bit like automobile insurance, in the respect that there is no return of premium if you don't need the insurance. You could sink hundreds of thousands of premium dollars into a policy, live a good long life, and "die with your boots on," so to speak, and never file a claim. On the one hand, you dodged the long-term care bullet. But on the other hand, those premium dollars are gone and they are not coming back. Your heirs will see nary a penny of

---

[45] LongTermCare.gov. 2017. "Who Needs Care?" https://longtermcare.acl.gov/the-basics/who-needs-care.html.

[46] National Bureau of Economic Research. Nov. 6, 2017. "The Market for Long-Term Care Insurance." http://www.nber.org/bah/winter05/w10989.html.

it, nor will they enjoy the investment value those premium dollars might have provided had they been wisely invested.

Nailing down the average cost of a traditional long-term-care insurance policy is tricky and complicated. Each company that offers the product will charge different rates and base the premiums on age, benefits, the length of time you want the company to pay the benefits and your health. The premium cost will also be affected by something called an "elimination period," which boils down to a deductible. The elimination period is the length of time you are willing to wait from when your care begins until your benefits start. You can add to the premium cost by choosing options to cover.

According to the American Association for Long-Term Care Insurance (AALTCI), a husband and wife, both age 60, will pay between $100 and $150 per month ($2,400 and $3,600 annually) for a "good" long-term-care insurance policy in 2017. The AALTCI breaks down the quality of coverage into three categories: good, better and best. The "good" category provides for only one year of coverage. That blanket of coverage is less than half what you will need if Professor Pfau's projection holds true that the average length of time people stay in a nursing home is 2.2 years.

If the goal of buying insurance is to remove financial risk, then it's a matter of balancing how much risk you can afford to take against the cost of removing (or reducing) the risk. [47, 48, 49, 50]

---

[47] Reviews.com. Jan. 20, 2017. "Life Insurance: The Best Long-Term Care Insurance." http://www.reviews.com/life-insurance/long-term-care.

[48] John Waggoner. USA Today. Dec. 2, 2013. "Long-term care insurance: Peace of mind at a price." https://www.usatoday.com/story/money/columnist/waggoner/2013/12/02/long-term-care-insurance/3807147.

[49] California Department of Insurance. Dec. 1, 2016. "2016 Long-Term Care Insurance." https://interactive.web.insurance.ca.gov/apex_extprd/f?p=111:40:::NO::P40_SEARCH:Y.

Alternative Solutions

One thing about the free-enterprise system that we can all cherish is it usually finds a way. Insurance companies are in business to make a profit. That's no big secret. All you have to do is pay attention the skyline of any major city and gaze upon the steel and glass towers owned by insurance giants. Inside the board rooms and think tanks of these large insurance companies are teams of actuaries and computer programmers whose job is to calculate ways of finding financial itches and creative ways to scratch them. This is certainly true of the long-term-care dilemma.

One of the most creative innovations to come along in recent years in this arena is the hybrid alternative to LTC insurance. This approach has also been called the "linked benefit" approach, and the "combo," because it combines either life insurance or annuity products with long-term-care benefits. They typically do this by sticking a rider to a life policy or annuity that, when triggered, pays a portion of the cost of long-term care. This is relatively new on the insurance scene, but seems to be gaining in popularity, especially among baby boomers who are just now coming face-to-face with the problem for themselves. Boomers, voting with their pocketbooks, tended to eschew the use-it-or-lose-it approach taken by traditional insurance. Another advantage to these hybrids is they often bypass underwriting, so health problems won't mean automatic rejection. Certain hybrids also feature tax advantages and fixed premiums, which means insulation against unexpected rate increases.

Some annuities can tack on a long-term-care rider that allows you to double the amount you are eligible to withdraw if you need, for example, nursing home care. The riders aren't free. They

---

[50] American Association for Long-Term Care Insurance. Feb. 5, 2016. "2016 Long Term Care Insurance Price Index Posted." http://www.aaltci.org/news/long-term-care-insurance-association-news/2016-long-term-care-insurance-price-index-posted.

cost a certain percent (typically under 1 percent) of the amount you deposit into the annuity, and you pay that amount every year.

Then there are the long-term-care annuities themselves. These products work like a fixed annuity, but with a long-term-care *multiplier* built in (no rider) so a portion of the internal return pays out long-term-care benefits. How much is paid out depends on the terms of the contract. For example, in one contract, the insurance company pays out 30 percent of the aggregate value of the policy over three years after the annuity account value is depleted. Let's say a policyholder owns a $100,000 annuity. The insurance company would, for example, pay out 300 percent of that amount over a two-year period should the policyholder need long-term care. In these annuities, the annuity owner uses the annuity value first before the long-term-care benefit kicks in.

The life insurance policies that pay long-term-care benefits are essentially paying what are termed "accelerated benefits," or "living benefits"—that is, they pay a portion of the policy's death benefit while you are still living.

As with anything else in the world of financial products, you need to make sure you understand every aspect of these policies before you sign anything. Get professional assistance and "look under the hood" before you buy. Make sure it fits your individual circumstances. As we have said before, and it bears repeating, no one's situation is exactly like yours, and no financial product or solution is a one-size-fits-all. It must fit just like a puzzle piece, or it doesn't fit at all.

That said, however, when people fail to address long-term-care funding in their financial planning, they are betting they will never need it. It's a little like walking across a six-lane interstate during heavy traffic. You may make it across unscathed, but the odds are not in your favor.[51]

---

[51] AARP. May 2016. "Understanding Long-Term Care Insurance." http://www.aarp.org/health/health-insurance/info-06-2012/understanding-long-term-care-insurance.html.

CHAPTER EIGHT

Leaving a Legacy

"Everyone must leave something behind when he dies, my grandfather said. A child or a book or a painting or a house or a wall built or a pair of shoes made. Or a garden planted. Something your hand touched some way so your soul has somewhere to go when you die, and when people look at that tree or that flower you planted, you're there."
~ *Ray Bradbury, Fahrenheit 451*

Along with celebrity comes fame and riches. At least that is the public perception. So, if anyone should be able to afford expert advice on estate planning, you would think the rich and famous would. But, alas, some of the most horrific estate messes have been created by people who are household names. Some of their blunders cost their heirs millions of dollars in lost inheritance, and years lost wrangling in the courts.

Andrew and Danielle Mayoras, a husband-and-wife attorney team, have compiled several examples of estate-planning mistakes made by celebrities and lessons we can learn from them in their book, *Trial and Heirs – Famous Fortune Fights!*

Following are just a few.

Celebrity: Prince

Estate Planning Mistake: Leaving no will

The death of pop legend Prince Rogers Nelson shocked the world in April 2016. He was relatively young at 57 years old. Because he left no will, it was left to a Minnesota judge to decide how to distribute approximately $300 million to those claiming to be Prince's relatives. Prince was not married at the time of his death, and his only child died at a week old.

When a rich celebrity dies without leaving a last will and testament, long-lost relatives come out of the woodwork. The world would soon find out that Prince had several half-siblings who came forward to stake their claim on not just the $300 million, but the royalties that could be generated by his published and unpublished music. He reportedly had thousands of songs he had never released. According to Minnesota law, a probate judge would have to decide the legitimacy of all claims to the estate—a task that is still ongoing as this book goes to press.

Celebrity: James Gandolfini

Mistake: Failure to address estate taxes

If you have ever watched the popular cable TV series *The Sopranos,* you are familiar with the lovable gangster portrayed by James Gandolfini. He died in June of 2013 of a heart attack while he was on vacation in Rome. Gandolfini, who was worth $70 million, had a will that left his fortune to his wife, daughter and two sisters, but the federal and state estate taxes claimed the lion's share of the money—55 percent. Could creating a trust have avoided such a big tax bite? Probably. "For many people, not just celebrities, a simple will is not enough," says Andrew Mayoras. "There are a lot of estate taxes that could have been avoided if he [Gandolfini] had done better estate planning, including a trust."

Celebrity: Marlon Brando
Mistake: Making oral promises

Who can forget actor Marlon Brando's performances on the big screen? He is legendary for yelling "Stella," in *A Streetcar Named Desire* and convincing the audience that he really was a gangster in *The Godfather.* Brando died in July 2004, leaving an estate of approximately $100 million. The problem was, his written estate plan didn't jibe with certain verbal commitments he allegedly made to Angela Borlaza, his housekeeper of many years. Borlaza sued the estate, claiming she was entitled to the house, which she said the actor had promised her. Even though Brando had never given the woman legal ownership, the housekeeper's attorneys went after the house and $2 million in punitive damages. The case was eventually settled for $125,000.

Celebrity: Michael Jackson
Mistake: Failure to fund a trust.

Michael Jackson, the "King of Pop," appeared to spend money as fast as he made it. When he died in June 2009 from a fatal concoction of prescription sleep medication, he was reported to be bankrupt. But his estate kept right on earning money. Sony reportedly paid Michael Jackson's estate $750 million in 2016 for the rights to a large catalog of music the singer had purchased when he was alive. According to Mayoras, one of Jackson's biggest estate-planning mistakes was creating a trust and then failing to fund it. Without a properly funded trust, an estate's beneficiaries must rely on the courts to settle things. "Probate court is public, more expensive, time-consuming and more prone to fighting," Mayoras says. To fund a trust, you must physically transfer your assets to the trust. That means changing titles and deeds from your individual name (or joint names, if married) to the name of your trust.

Celebrity: Heath Ledger

Mistake: Inadvertently omitting a child

Heath Ledger was such a good actor that when he portrayed "The Joker" in the Batman series, *The Dark Knight,* he even scared his fellow actors on the set. As professional as he was in life, however, he failed to update an old will and inadvertently disinherited a daughter, Matilda, age 2 at the time of his death of an accidental drug overdose in 2008. Ledger's entire $20 million estate went to his parents and his three sisters. This was probably not his intentions. To avoid this mistake, your will should include language that includes not only named children, but also any children, natural or adopted, or children you will have in the future—even stepchildren.

Celebrity: Philip Seymour Hoffman

Mistake: Not using trusts

Philip Seymour Hoffman was an actor/director/producer best known for his character roles on the big screen. He portrayed author Truman Capote in the movie *Capote* in 2005. Hoffman said he was determined "not to let his children turn into spoiled 'trust-fund kids'," so he avoided trusts in his estate-planning choices. When he was found dead of an apparent drug overdose in his Manhattan, New York, home in 2014, he was worth an estimated $35 million, all of which went to Marianne O'Donnell, the mother of his three children. "That might not have been so bad," writes Mayoras, "except that Hoffman's decision meant his beneficiaries also inherited a whopper of an estate tax bill." Mayoras also said that Hoffman's opinion about trusts automatically creating a lazy, entitled trust-fund kids was not correct. "Trusts can be customized, and Hoffman could have made specific stipulations about when, how and under what circumstances his kids inherited money—including a provision that the children work," Mayoras said.

Celebrity: Florence Griffith Joyner
Mistake: Keeping a will's location secret
They called her "Flo Jo." She was an Olympic gold medalist, perhaps best known for her track skills. She took home the silver medal in the 200-meter event at the Los Angeles, California, 1984 Olympic Games. She died at age 38 of an apparent seizure in 1998. Florence Griffith Joyner had a will but no one knew where she kept it. That meant her estate would have to be settled in probate court—a costly, public process that required four years. The lesson here is to take either a trusted close relative or a financial professional, or both, into your confidence about the location of your important personal documents.[52, 53]

Celebrity: Marilyn Monroe
Mistake: Not thoroughly designating beneficiaries
When you name your beneficiaries in a will, be thorough and specific. Your wealth may end up in someone else's hands if you aren't. Take the case of Marilyn Monroe. When she died of a drug overdose in 1962, she had a will that left money to care for her mentally ill mother, and she left some personal items to people who were close friends. She left the bulk of her estate to her acting coach, Lee Strasberg. But Marilyn probably had no idea how much money her estate would continue to earn after her death. Lee Strasberg died in 1982, leaving his 75 percent interest in the Monroe estate to his second wife, Anna, someone whom Marilyn had barely known. Anna knew a good thing when she saw it. She took over the rights to Marilyn's name and image and made millions.

---

[52] Lynnette Khalfani-Cox. AARP. 2016. "Celebrity Estate Planning Mistakes." https://www.aarp.org/money/taxes/info-2016/celebrity-estate-mistakes-photo.html#slide1

[53] Andrew W Mayoras and Danielle B. Mayoras. Wise Circle Books. Nov. 1, 2012. "Trial & Heirs: Famous Fortune Fights!"

Over the years since her death, Marilyn's name and image has appeared on everything from clothing to coffee mugs, and every time it does, it makes a profit for someone who was not in her will.

According to "The Balance," a wills and estate planning website, Marilyn Monroe's estate remained open until 2001 when the New York Surrogate Court finally declared the estate completely settled and authorized transfer of the remaining assets of the estate to Marilyn Monroe LLC, a Delaware limited liability company, managed by Anna Strasberg. In 2010, the LLC was acquired by Authentic Brands Group and NECA for an estimated $50 million, which in turn formed a company named The Estate of Marilyn Monroe LLC. "The Balance" reports the estate continues to generate about $15 million per year, only behind the estates of Michael Jackson and Elvis Presley.[54]

The lesson from this is simple: Be specific about whom you wish to inherit your wealth. Bestow your assets in such a manner that they will pass "per stirpes"—or equally among the branches of your family. For example, if you name your two adult children as beneficiaries of your IRA, and if one of them precedes you in death, you may want that child's portion to go to his or her children.

Finally, update your will and the beneficiary forms in your important documents with each life event, such as divorce, remarriage, births and deaths. Remember also the name that appears on the beneficiary line of a financial document trumps a provision made in a will. We could tell you horror stories of people who placed the name of a current spouse on the beneficiary line of an IRA and forgot all about it. Meanwhile, a divorce and remarriage ensued. Wills were updated, but not the beneficiary line on the

---

[54] Julie Garber. The Balance. May 1, 2017. "Summary of Marilyn Monroe's Last Will and Testament." https://www.thebalance.com/marilyn-monroe-will-testament-3505094.

IRA. Hundreds of thousands of dollars ended up in the bank accounts of the children of the ex-spouse's new partner—people to whom the deceased had no family connection whatsoever.

Terri Schiavo was not a celebrity, but her name became synonymous with what can happen if you don't have a living will.

On Feb. 25, 1990, 41-year-old Terri Schiavo collapsed in her home in Florida and was rushed to the hospital suffering from a potassium imbalance. Unfortunately, her brain was deprived of oxygen for more than five minutes and she lay in what doctors called a "persistent vegetative state" for more than a decade. That meant she wasn't brain-dead, but she couldn't speak, think or respond to commands. She was kept alive through a feeding tube.

The matter ended up in Florida courts, with her parents wanting her kept alive artificially, hoping she would come around, and Terri's husband, Michael, arguing it was her wish not to be kept alive by artificial means. This was never put in writing, however, and the matter dragged on until 2005 when the parents lost their last legal appeal.

Had there existed a document expressing Terri Schiavo's wishes, of course, the family and the nation could have been spared a heart-wrenching ordeal.[55]

The "Evils" of Probate

In California, if you die with assets of more than $150,000, and you have only a will and no estate plan, you may be leaving behind a lot of trouble for your loved ones. By assets, we mean anything of value: cash in the bank, real estate, stocks, bonds, businesses, rental property. Essentially, anything that does not have a desig-

---

[55] CNN Law Center. March 25, 2005. "Background on the Schiavo case." http://www.cnn.com/2005/LAW/03/25/schiavo.qa.

nated beneficiary. Don't get us wrong. You need to have a will. But if you have no estate plan, the chances are good your estate will land in probate court and a judge will have to settle it.

Time-Consuming

What's wrong with the probate process? Well, for one thing, it is slow. Why does probate take so long in California? The process is governed by something called "probate code," which determines, among other things, time frame. You first have to file a petition. Then, after two or three months, you receive a date for your first hearing. At that time, the executor of the estate is named. Then, notices to creditors (anyone who may have a legal claim against the estate) must be notified. After public notification, creditors have 60 days to file a claim. Meanwhile, the estate must be evaluated by professional auditors. Items must be counted, categorized and a value placed on them. Next, assets will be liquidated, if necessary, to pay debts and taxes. All of that takes time. Finally, after all that red tape has been untangled, the remaining assets are left to the family.

If everything goes smoothly, average time is at least a year. But we have heard of horror stories of probate cases dragging on for five years or more. What could cause such delays? Multiple beneficiaries, for one. Sometimes, much time is devoted to tracking down long-lost beneficiaries who are never located. Sometimes the validity of a will is contested. That requires filing a complaint with the court. Then depositions must be taken and filed. A contested will can end up in either mediation or a courtroom trial. All that takes time.

In some probate proceedings, emotions run high and family members wrangle over such things as who should be the administrator of the estate, the qualification of beneficiaries, the valuation of property within the estate, and on and on. These disagreements must be handled through attorneys, who charge hefty hourly fees. Motions and petitions filed before the court take time. Naturally, the more complicated the estate, the more time-consuming the process. If the estate contains a business, for example, and that business owes taxes and owns property, then a detailed appraisal must be performed and tax obligations must be sorted out before the value of the estate can be distributed by heirs. [56]

Costly

The California legislature has seen fit to regulate how much attorneys can charge for representing your estate in probate proceedings, but it still isn't cheap. According to the state Probate Code section 10810, there is a descending scale that goes as follows:

(1) 4 percent on the first $100,000.
(2) 3 percent on the next $100,000.
(3) 2 percent on the next $800,000.
(4) 1 percent on the next $9,000,000.
(5) 0.5 percent on the next $15,000,000.
(6) For all amounts above $25,000,000, a reasonable amount to be determined by the court.

If the case is complicated by such things as lawsuits or tax problems—and many of them are—the court can allow higher fees. So, if the average probate process costs 5 percent of the estate's gross value, then a $1 million house going through probate would cost

---

[56] Roy M. Doppelt. Estate Planning Source. Sept. 14, 2012. "Why Does Probate Take So Long? (In California)." theestateplanningsource.com/why-does-probate-take-so-long-in-california.

$50,000. Add to that figure if legal complications, such as easement disputes or other litigations, arise.[57]

It comes down to this: Which is more expensive? Estate planning or probate? Hands down, probate is more expensive by leaps and bounds. Not to mention the fact that your family is more at peace and knows exactly what to expect. With an estate plan in place, they can also honor your wishes and get on with their lives after your demise.

Loss of Privacy

Like most court proceedings, probate is open to the public. According to legalzoom.com, you can view all the details of a will with even the most sensitive and personal information by simply going to the courthouse, walking into the county clerk's office, and asking for the file. There you can find out the names and addresses of all the beneficiaries and a complete list of what the estate consisted of. You can even make copies if you want.

That means anybody can see how much you left to whom. Would it surprise you to learn there are people out there who track such information? They scour the newspapers where advertisements of probate proceedings are required to appear. These predators know who to pick on. Sometimes minors are mentioned in wills and inherit large sums of money when they come of age. Do you know of any young men or women who, if they had large sums of cash at their disposal, might make bad decisions? Or be easy prey for hucksters and con artists? Or how about widows or

---

[57] California Legislative Information. "ARTICLE 2. Compensation of Attorney for the Personal Representative [10810 - 10814]." https://leginfo.legislature.ca.gov/faces/codes_displayText.xhtml?lawCode=PROB&division=7.&title=&part=7.&chapter=1.&article=2.

widowers whose judgement might a bit diminished after experiencing the trauma of losing their mate?

What Can You Do?

So, what can you do to avoid the evils of probate? Consult a qualified financial advisor who works with an attorney and look into the possible advantages of living trusts. Check on the advisability of a transfer on death (TOD) account, which is a special type of investment account that allows for assets to be transferred upon the death of the owner directly to a previously named beneficiary. Typically, all you need to access such a bequeathed account is to provide the custodian of the investment account a valid death certificate of the original owner.

The owner of the account retains control over it while he or she is alive, and the beneficiary will not have access unless specifically granted by the owner. If competent, the owner, while living, can also change the beneficiary at any time.[58]

California Gov. Jerry Brown signed Assembly Bill 139 on Sept. 21, 2015, which cleared the way for the state's property owners to transfer real property upon their deaths and avoid probate. The document you need to accomplish this is a "revocable transfer on death deed." It is relatively simple to obtain and does not require a living trust.[59]

Payable on death (POD) accounts allow banks to pass on the proceeds of checking and savings accounts, CDs, money market accounts and U.S. savings bonds to a named beneficiary, thus keeping the assets out of probate.

---

[58] Julie Garber. The Balance. Nov. 1, 2017. "How to Avoid Probate with a Transfer on Death Account (TOD)." https://www.thebalance.com/what-is-a-transfer-on-death-or-tod-account-3505253.

[59] A People's Choice. 2016. "New California Transfer on Death Deed." https://apeopleschoice.com/california-transfer-on-death-deed

Joint tenants with right of survivorship (JTWROS) is a designation that allows for joint owners to own and access an account equally and assume complete legal control of the account should one of the owners die. It is sometimes called tenancy by entirety. Why is it useful? Suppose Tom and Bill own a house at the beach. If the ownership documents specify JTWROS, then either Tom or Bill automatically own the home if the other dies *without having to go through probate.*[60]

Finally, make sure your documents are up to date. Remember designated beneficiaries are generally immune to contestability and probate proof, but you must make sure your documents are up to date.

---

[60] Investing Answers. "Joint Tenants with Right of Survivorship (JTWROS)." http://www.investinganswers.com/financial-dictionary/est.ate-planning/joint-tenants-right-survivorship-jtwros-3490.

CHAPTER NINE

Investing Myths and Misconceptions

"The great enemy of the truth is very often not the lie, deliberate, contrived and dishonest, but the myth, persistent, persuasive and unrealistic."

~ *John F. Kennedy*

Have you noticed investment advice is everywhere these days? Has everyone you know turned financial Dutch uncle on you? Has your 8-year-old grandchild been giving you stock tips? Does your next-door neighbor think he is the reincarnated Nostradamus of Wall Street?

In the 1990s, you could do no wrong in the stock market. Some people call it the "curse of the good times." In those days, you could have taken the Wall Street Journal, spread it on the wall, thrown a dart at the mutual fund page, invested in wherever the point landed, and realized a 25–30 percent return. Even though those days are gone, we are amazed at how many people invest on hunches, gut instincts and rumors.

Check out the magazine section of any large book store and you will find scores of magazines devoted to investment advice. These slick-paper periodicals, each competing to tell you what you should do with your money, post attention-grabbing headlines such as:

"Gold – The New Investment Frontier"
"Great Depression Dead Ahead"
"Why the Dollar Will Soar"
"Why the Dollar Will Fall"
"Oil and Gas Investors in for a Windfall"

You can find validation in print for just about any investment philosophy you wish to believe in these days by writers who swear by their sources.

Seekers of truth recognize, however, there are no absolutes when it comes to building wealth and managing it. There is nearly always an alternative viewpoint. What is true and valid for one portfolio and one investor may not work for another.

But those magazines won't tell you that. It would be difficult to sell magazines with boring (but true) headlines like:

"Your Individual Goals Should Determine Your Investment Choices."

Or

"Many Factors Should Determine How Much Investment Risk You Take On."

The reason why the print media opts for the sensational is because it moves the merchandise. Have you ever seen a newspaper headline that read: *"Nothing Went on Today That Is Worth Mentioning?"* Neither have we.

The point is, it's not a good idea to make decisions on your future based on investment tips shouted from magazine covers. They are mostly entertainment. Thumb through the advertisement section of the magazine and you can get a good idea of who is influencing the articles. So, unless you have just disembarked on the last load of cantaloupes, you know better than to trust everything you read or hear.

Financial Television

Cable TV has led to the proliferation of financial channels where talking heads dispense an endless stream of stock tips and up-to-the-minute Wall Street goings on. Each swing of the market up or down is given a cause-and-effect explanation, some of which appear logical while others seem conjured out of thin air.

We confess to watching the financial channels from time to time. Not to learn anything, you understand, but to be entertained. One program likes to put two "analysts" on the screen, each with an opposing view, and let them over-talk each other in an interview conducted by someone who eggs them on. It's the "Jerry Springer Show" of financial programming.

Then there is the guy who comes on with his sleeves rolled up, wearing a funny hat, who punctuates investment advice with sound effects. On one show we watched, he had a bicycle horn and a slide whistle.

He screams, "I told you people out there two weeks ago that (insert stock symbol here) was going to take off, but you didn't listen!" Then he brings on a caller, probably screened to make sure he is not a heckler, to ask a set-up question.

We did say this was entertainment, didn't we? But the problem is, people make investment decisions based on his rantings and ravings. When he gets lucky and (insert stock symbol here) actually does take off, people start to believe he is omniscient. The truth is, you seldom hear when his bold predictions are wrong.

One of the most egregious bad calls this guy ever made was shortly before the collapse of the large investment bank, Bear Stearns, in 2008. On March 11, 2008, he screamed at the television audience in his hyperbolic style, "No! No! No! Bear Stearns is not in trouble. If anything, they're more likely to be taken over. Don't move your money from Bear."

Three days later, on March 14, 2008, Bear Stearns stock fell 92 percent on news of a Fed bailout and $2-a-share takeover by JPMorgan."[61]

All we're saying is, please take it all with a huge grain of salt and understand it for what it is… entertainment. We would even call it comedy if it weren't for the fact that some unwary investors have risked their money on such calls and lost.

The Water-Cooler Analyst

If you've ever worked in an office, you have probably met the "water-cooler analyst." This is the co-worker who wants to let you in on the ground floor of an investment opportunity. Or maybe they know someone who knows someone, who has a friend who knows about an IPO about to explode (as in, "go up in value times 10 and make you tons of money"). The next Google. These phenomena are called "hot stock tips," and what makes them so tempting is the idea you can "pull one over on those fat cats on Wall Street" and beat the system.

We have found such hot investment advice is generally worth exactly what you pay for it—nothing.

Well-Meaning Relatives and Friends

Some of the worst investment advice comes from friends and relatives who are trying to be helpful. It's obvious why people take

---

[61] Lou Carlozo. MSN.com. March 4, 2016. "10 of the worst Wall Street calls in history." http://www.msn.com/en-us/money/savingandinvesting/10-of-the-worst-wall-street-calls-in-history/ss-AAgt2XX.

this advice. They trust their family and friends and assume, usually correctly, they are not driven by some profit motive. It is human nature to make emotional decisions and defend them with logic. When Uncle Joe or your cousin Bob whispers in your ear at the Thanksgiving roundup about his success (or anticipated success) with (fill in ticker symbol here), your inclination is to give it at least a measure of credence without checking the facts. Here at the offices of BML Wealth Management, we review portfolios every day, and you would be amazed at how many of them contain an equity purchase here and there that originated from just such a recommendation—and how few of them pan out.

Scams and Con Artists

The water-cooler people and friends and relatives are well-meaning, but there are some con artists out there whose dastardly schemes are artfully designed to separate you from your money. One such scheme we have come across is called the "pump-it-up-and-dump-it" scam. Here's how it works. You're at your computer. An email pops up. It's in your inbox, but it appears to be intended for someone else. This is an intentional case of mistaken identity. That is what pulls you in. The message may read something like this:

"Hey Freddy. What's up? Please don't tell anybody about this, or I could get into big, big trouble, but this stock is about to sky rocket...etcetera, etcetera, yada, yada." The message might conclude with "Please say hello to the wife and kids."

Your name is not Freddy, but still, you can't help but read it. The perpetrators of this little scheme hope you will be intrigued and act on the information. What you don't know is they have probably sent out thousands of these messages to random email addresses. Their objective is to inflate the price of a penny (microcap) stock, then dump their own shares when the price goes up, and leave you holding the bag when investors learn the hard way it's all a scam.

It has been our observation that these rats seem to scamper out of the cellar during market downturns. These email schemes are the electronic version of "pump-and-dump" voice messages and bulk mail.

"Hello, this is Eugene at ABC Brokerage Firm," the voice may say. "Just calling to let you know XYZ stock is going up 200 percent next week. Say hi to the wife."

Most people are too savvy to be taken in. But these scammers figure there are enough poor saps who are tripped up by their own greed to fall for the ruse. And they are right. FINRA (the Financial Industry Regulatory Authority) says just delete any text or email that sounds like this, and hang up on and disregard any such voice message.[62]

Timing the Market

"Buy low and sell high" is perhaps the oldest piece of investing advice around. The more sophisticated term for it is "value investing." The idea is to buy stocks when they are "on sale," hold them until the price goes up, and sell at just the right time—before the share price retreats. There's only one problem. No one—and we mean no one—has a crystal ball. No one can predict what the stock market will do from one day to the next.

But hold on a second! Can't analysts predict the market? Isn't that what all the charts and fund ratings are all about? The short answer is no.

---

[62] FINRA. Sept. 2, 2015. "Messaging Apps are Latest Platform for Delivering Pump-and-Dump Scams." http://www.finra.org/investors/alerts/messaging-apps-scams.

We all have 20-20 hindsight. Those analysts who give mutual funds their ratings are looking at past performance. The funds you will hear the most about are the ones that have four-star and five-star ratings issued to them by financial research companies such as Morningstar. But not even they can see into the future. All the rating system does is identify the few funds that performed well in the past. Each year, mutual funds that were once winners disappear from the list and are never heard of again.

Markets, by their very nature, are unpredictable and given to sudden, unexpected changes. In his book, *Unconventional Success – A Fundamental Approach to Personal Investment,* David Swensen wrote: "Overwhelmingly, mutual funds extract enormous sums from investors in exchange for providing a shocking disservice."[63]

Swensen is chief investment officer at Yale University. In 2011, he wrote an opinion piece for the *New York Times* in which he called out mutual funds for, as he put it, "delivering inferior results." Swensen wrote: "For decades, the mutual fund industry, which manages more than $13 trillion for 90 million Americans, has employed market volatility to produce profits for itself far more reliably than it has produced returns for its investors. Too often, investors believe that mutual funds provide a safe haven, placing a misguided trust in brokers, advisers and fund managers. In fact, the industry has a history of delivering inferior results to investors, and its regulators do not provide effective oversight."

Companies that manage mutual funds continue to perpetuate the myth that certain fund managers are imbued with the gift of prescience and can time the market. But fund managers must produce profits for their owners. Swensen points out fund managers often buy and sell within the funds they manage to increase their compensation. In the *Times* opinion piece, he says "in 2010, investors redeemed $152 billion from one-star, two-star and three-star

---

[63] David F. Swensen. Simon &Schuster. August 2005. "Unconventional Success."

funds and placed $304 billion in four-star and five-star funds." According to Swensen, this goes on year in and year out. The churning of investor portfolios benefits only the churners, not the mutual fund owners. Actually, since the mutual fund industry uses the star-rating system to encourage performance-chasing (selling funds that performed poorly and buying funds that performed well), investors end up actually buying low and selling high—which is exactly the opposite of the formula for trading success![64]

"Welcome to where nearly everyone is below average," began the article in *USA Today*, April 25, 2017. "It's the world where investors try to pick which mutual funds will beat the market. It sounds great in theory, but the odds of doing it successfully over the long term can be slimmer than winning a lotto prize." The writer, Stan Choi of the Associated Press, says when you measure the performance of mutual funds against indexes in various categories, a disappointing picture emerges.[65]

"Most funds did poorly relative to their index, and not just ones that focus on U.S. stocks, whose performance has been getting the heaviest scrutiny. The majority of bond funds and foreign stock funds also failed to keep pace with their indexes for the 15 years through 2016."

You know that little thing golfers do on the green when they are studying their putt? They take a few tufts of grass and toss them in the air to see which way the breeze is blowing. There are some golfers who think this is pointless. It measures the wind 10 feet higher than the ball, for one thing. For another, if you have to toss grass into the air to see the wind, then it's probably not that much of a factor. Lastly, it measures *that* puff of wind, at *that* mo-

---

[64] David F. Swensen, New York Times. Aug. 14, 2011. "Opinion: The Mutual Fund Merry-Go-Round." http://www.nytimes.com/2011/08/14/opinion/sunday/the-mutual-fund-merry-go-round.html.

[65] Stan Choi. USA Today reprinted from The Associated Press. April 25, 2017. "Where Nearly Everyone Is Below Average: Investing in Mutual Funds." https://www.usatoday.com/story/money/personalfinance/2017/04/25/where-nearly-everyone-below-average-investing-funds/100716954/.

ment. Puffs of wind are subject to the whim and fancy of air currents and can change accordingly. Likewise, the stock market moves up, down and sideways without predictability. Anyone who tells you they can time the market is lying to you.

Judy Sheindlin, the famous "Judge Judy" of television, wrote a book about her experiences in the reality courtroom series over which she presides. We haven't read the book, but the title grabbed our attention: *Don't Pee on My Leg and Tell Me It's Raining.* Some myths and misconceptions about money and investing are obviously dubious. Others are die-hard urban legends are so deeply etched into our national economic consciousness that it takes a crowbar to dislodge them. We expect shady dealings from pushy salespeople, but, if you are like us, you deeply resent it when so-called experts who bill themselves as stewards of the public trust throw us a curve ball.

The Latin phrase *caveat emptor* ("Let the buyer beware") comes to mind. Any time money is involved, it is incumbent on individual investors to do their due diligence before signing anything. You worked hard for your money. When you retire and sever yourself from the umbilical paycheck, your accumulated wealth may still work for you, but you will probably be depleting it at a rate faster than it can be replenished. In other words, it becomes a nonrenewable resource. That's why we recommend you at least obtain a second opinion, and always check out the facts before stepping off into territory unfamiliar to you.

CHAPTER TEN

Eight Investing Mistakes Retirees Make and How You Can Avoid Them

"Keep your eyes on the ball," said the golf coach. "Each time you swing, you are looking up to see where the ball goes, and it is affecting your shot."

Golf pros will tell you moving your head in the backswing of a tee shot is one of the most common mistakes golfers make. It may seem like a simple thing, but hours of practice are often necessary to correct it.

Investing for and in retirement comes with its own list of don'ts that must be pointed out. If you are a golfer, mistakes on the tee box will merely put your ball in the rough and make your second shot difficult. Investing mistakes can cost you thousands of dollars. Wealth forfeited through poor judgment or bad advice can make the difference between enjoying a worry-free retirement and struggling through your golden years. Following is the list of a few of the most common traps and how to avoid them.

Mistake #1: Investing as if You Were Still Working

If you are like most people, during your working years, you invested for your future retirement through some type of retirement plan, usually a 401(k), 403(b), IRA or something similar. In most of these plans, you had a "menu" of investment choices. You could select a variety of mutual funds. You may have had a variety of stock funds, bond funds or money market accounts. Some plans may have allowed you to invest in company stock at a discount.

Most retirement plans had a big financial company like Fidelity or Vanguard as a custodian. You may have interacted with this institution's advisors for decades. Perhaps you became familiar with the retirement plan's website.

Over the years, as retirement loomed closer, what changes did you make in the way your investments were placed within the retirement plan? Most people we talk to say they made few, if any, changes to their portfolios. At most, some may have positioned more of their holdings into bond funds and less into stock funds as they approached retirement. Is that the case with you?

Retirement represents a fundamental change in your personal life. You will be drawing the curtain closed on your working years and entering a new phase where you can pursue your favorite hobby, travel, play with the grandchildren or work on your golf game. You are also entering a new financial phase of life, too. You are leaving accumulation mode and entering the preservation and distribution modes. It only stands to reason that your investing perspective must change.

Let's say you are 45 years old, and you are sitting down with one of the 401(k) plan's advisor representatives to allocate your investments. Your risk tolerance is appropriately high, as you have 20 more years before retirement. The advisor says you need a blend of growth stocks, international stocks, small cap stocks and large cap stocks. That's probably appropriate, too. Does it matter if the stock market goes up and down? Not really. When it goes up, that's good! The balance in your account goes up. When it goes down, that's good, too. Shares are less expensive, and your contribution is buying more of them. When the market goes back up (as it always does in time) those skinny shares will fatten up, and you will be ahead of the game.

Fast forward a few years. Now, you are in your 60s, edging ever closer to retirement. Time, which used to be an investing ally, is no longer on your side. Those regular contributions you are making to your 401(k) will soon cease when you sever yourself from your paycheck. Remember the dollar-cost-averaging strategy that worked so well for you during your working years? Well, that stops working for you. In fact, a downturn in the stock market now could represent a loss for which there is no counterbalance.

Here's another problem that may arise: Your advisor tells you, now you are approaching retirement, you need to move from mutual funds into bonds to mitigate risk. As we write this book, bonds and bond funds have had a great 30-year run. Why? Because interest rates have been lower than any time in recent history. Bonds go up in value when interest rates go down, and vice versa. But when interest rates have been at historic lows, they have only one direction to go. The inverse relationship between bonds and interest rates could work against your financial fortunes—and at the worst possible time if you are entering retirement. Does putting money into bonds or bond funds guarantee safety when you are about to retire? Which way do you think interest rates will go in the future? Up or down? There's your answer.

There is one more element about investing in bonds we would be remiss not to mention. Just because a bond is issued by a "government" does not mean iron-clad security. Backers of some municipal bonds default. The following headline appeared April 22, 2016, in the *New York Times*: "Municipal Bond Defaults Shake Up a Once-Sedate Market." It listed several municipal bonds that had been in the news for all the wrong reasons, "starting with places like Jefferson County, Alabama, and Stockton, California, defaulting on their municipal bonds. Then Detroit filed for bankruptcy, with $18 billion in debt on its books."

The article continued: "And there's Puerto Rico, which is struggling to make its bond payments—or decide which of its $72 billion in municipal bonds to default on."[66]

Recessions affect municipalities just as they do individuals. When the flow of revenue is reduced, something must give. In recent years, many counties and cities across the nation have had to decide between supplying basic services and meeting their bond obligations. Sometimes it comes down to whose voices are heard. Will it be the voices of investors who bought the bonds, or the voices of angry citizens whose garbage cans are overflowing and are not receiving basic municipal services?

Painting a Chevy Doesn't Make It a Ford

When advisors working for large companies administering employer retirement plans give the same kind of advice to people in their 60s as they do to people in their 40s, serious problems can develop. Moving from one mutual fund to another still puts you in mutual funds. You can take a Chevy, give it a new paint job and call it a Ford, but it's still a Chevy. Moving money from one mutual fund into another in the interest of safety is activity, but not necessarily accomplishment. The mix may be different, but the assets of the account holder are still at risk. Cash, or money market funds, are safe all right. But when it comes to returns, they are like slow-moving streams. The interest received from these alloca-

---

[66] Paul Sullivan. New York Times. April 22, 2016. "Municipal Bond Defaults Shake Up a Once-Sedate Market." https://www.nytimes.com/2016/04/23/your-money/municipal-bond-defaults-shake-up-a-once-sedate-market.html.

tions is not enough to keep up with inflation, even when it is at its lowest.

Investing Tradeoffs

Life is full of tradeoffs. So is investing.

In Southern California, where we work and live, you can negotiate through traffic on busy freeways to get to a Sam's Club or a Costco. When you get there, good luck finding a parking place near the entrance or a short line at checkout. But you must admit, the prices are lower. They have the little shop around the corner beat in that category, especially if you don't mind buying in bulk.

We once saw this sign posted above the cash register at a small, family-owned hardware store whose business was being threatened by a new megastore down the street: *"Great Quality, Low Prices, Fantastic Service – Pick Any TWO!"* Yes, you save money in the super stores, but the lower prices drive in more customers, all of whom park cars and clog aisles—a factor that diminishes the overall shopping experience.

In finance, you have similar tradeoffs.

When it comes to where you can invest, there are essentially three "worlds," each of which has certain desirable characteristics: **SAFE WORLD, RISK WORLD** and **HYBRID WORLD.** Let's look at them one at a time.

SAFE WORLD – As the name implies, you have complete safety of principal in this world. Banks live here. Ask a banker where to put your money where it is safe and will have a good rate of return, and he or she will likely point you in the direction of certificates of deposit. CDs come in different sizes, anywhere from one to five years in length. As we write this, CD interest rates are low—around 1 or 2 percent, and there is a penalty for early withdrawal.

The government also does business in this world. They will no doubt point you to their Treasury bonds. Returns here are also low, but, again, your money is perfectly safe from loss.

Insurance companies do business in SAFE WORLD. They will point you to fixed annuities where the rates are fixed and you know what your principal is from day to day. Interest is predictable and can often be calculated daily. Rates of return are usually a known quantity and terms are published. Small penalties for early withdrawal are set out in writing. This is the *known* world. The potential returns of traditional fixed annuities are typically better than that of CDs, ranging, as this is written, from 1-4 percent over a 12-month period.

RISK WORLD provides an excellent environment for growth but comes with an element of danger. Proponents of RISK WORLD will say, "No risk—no reward." As the term implies, you can lose your money when you enter here.

Mutual funds are among the biggest players in RISK WORLD. Suppose you sit down with a mutual fund advisor—let's call him "Mr. Vanguard," and tell him that you have $50,000 to invest. Where do you suppose they will tell you to put it? Did you say in the family of mutual funds he represents? Bingo! What's wrong with that? Perhaps nothing, if that is what is best for you. But that depends on many factors—your age, your proximity to retirement, your goals, aims, desires and risk tolerance.

But don't expect objectivity from an advisor who is a captive broker. After all, you don't walk into a Chevy dealership to buy a Ford. And if you walk into an Apple computer store, don't be shocked if they want to sell you an Apple product. Brokers are denizens of RISK WORLD. This includes captive brokers, such as Smith Barney, Merrill Lynch, J.G. Edwards, etc. Independent advisors also work in this world, and can recommend strategies that work best for the client, irrespective of company affiliation.

In RISK WORLD, you can buy stocks, bonds, mutual funds, options, even real estate. Variable annuities are also part of RISK WORLD, as they are market-based products in an insurance wrapper. Variable annuities involve fees between 3 percent and 4.5 percent of their account values, not to mention "sub-account" fees, "rider" fees and "mortality and expense" fees.

RISK WORLD is the world of the unknown, where neither the principal nor earnings are guaranteed and the term is usually open-ended.

Then there is **HYBRID WORLD**—this is the middle world. It is a newer world than the other two, having been discovered in the last two decades or so. Its main characteristic—and, we think, its most meritorious characteristic—is it offers some of the best of the other two worlds. Denizens of this universe include banks and insurance companies.

Banks offer something called equity-linked certificates of deposit (ELCDs). These vehicles guarantee safety of principal while allowing investors to attach their rate of growth to the growth of the stock market. How do they do that? The ELCD is linked to a basket of stocks using an index, such as the S&P 500, Dow Jones or Nasdaq. This allows the investor to take advantage of the gains of the market *up to a point*, without risk of loss.

In HYBRID WORLD, insurance companies offer annuities that work on the same principle of the ELCD—principal protection with the opportunity to benefit from the upside of the market *up to a cap*. This annuity is neither the variable annuity, which is invested directly in the market, and can lose, nor is it the traditional fixed annuity, which has fixed interest rates. This hybrid annuity is known as a fixed index annuity (FIA). Growth, while potentially much greater than traditional fixed annuities, is not guaranteed. Your return could be as low as zero in a bad year, or as high as the insurance company's declared cap in a year when the market soars. FIAs have safety and growth potential, but the tradeoff is a measure of liquidity. Just like the sign in the hardware store said, "Pick any two." To have the greater growth potential, the term for FIAs is typically 10 years. Insurance companies, sensitive to the need for liquidity, usually provide a 10 percent free withdrawal per year during the 10-year surrender period, and arrange for a surrender penalty averaging approximately 12 percent to start with and then declining to zero by the 10th year. Keep in mind, there are as many FIA designs out there as there are car models. So, if an FIA is a possible solution for your financial retirement goals, check with your advisor for the one that offers the best fit for your individual situation.

How Much Should Go Where?

When we speak at seminars and educational workshops about retirement planning, we often observe all too often retirees have too much of their wealth invested in RISK WORLD. That's no problem with the market is up, but when pronounced downturns hit, we see some sad faces in the crowd. Many who have had what they considered to be moderate portfolios lost considerable chunks of their life's savings in these severe corrections.

So, how much should go where? It is healthy to have some money in all three of these worlds, and the answer to the "how much" question is, "it depends." As we have said repeatedly in this book, there is no one-size-fits-all pat answer that works, and anyone who has a cookie-cutter formula for how much money you should have in each of the three worlds is just whistling in the dark. Age is a big factor. So is risk tolerance. Your own personal goals must be considered. What do you want your money to do for you?

As we make our rounds in the financial planning world, we see some disturbing things. One is just how many people are skating on thin ice and not aware of it. Some drift over to where the thin ice is by not paying attention. Others have relied on direction from financial professionals who are limited in their training and experience. These financial advisors may have only one tool in their financial tool bo, and use it as a solution for each planning problem. As Abraham Maslow said, "If you only have a hammer, you tend to see every problem as a nail." Some financial professionals who work for big brokerage houses may be well-meaning, but they pound the square peg into the round hole over and over because it's all they have to work with.

Mistake #2: Not Protecting Yourself from Market Drops

In Chapter Two of this book, we discussed the "Rule of 100" and acknowledged that, while it is not a hard and fast rule to be set in stone, it is a good guide as to how you should consider distributing your risk as you age. The principle is, take your age, subtract it from 100, and the result will tell you approximately how much of your portfolio should be at risk. The remainder, of course, should be protected from loss. Alternately, you can put a percent sign after your age, and that's approximately how much you should have in safety. Either way works. The idea is, as you age, you should be taking on less risk. The reason is simple. As you age, the market will still ebb and flow, but you don't have time to ride out the waves and make up for losses.

So, does that mean if you are age 65, you should have approximately 65 percent of your money in "safe" products, and you can take reasonable risks with the other 35 percent? In a word, yes. But remember, next year you will be 66. So, it will be time to tweak and rebalance.

The phrase "risk tolerance" means just what it says. It's a comfort factor. To illustrate, two friends visit a sauna. On entering, one friend twists the temperature knob all the way up to the maximum. They both sit and swelter, enjoying the heat, making small talk as the temperature climbs. But one of the two friends grows more and more uncomfortable. Suddenly, he lunges for the door and heads for the sweet relief of the cold shower.

Just how much can you tolerate when an investment account is losing money you worked hard all your life to save? Can you stand to watch the stock ticker take more and more of your hard-earned wealth away with every passing hour? When your broker says, "Just hang in there; it will come back," at what point do you want to punch him in the nose? When day after day goes by and no comeback materializes, and you watch more and more of your life slide away with the plunging market reports, how do you feel? That's risk tolerance. How much can you stand? Each one of us is different. Only you can say how much risk is too much risk for you.

Which Tools Are "Safe?"

So, which financial tools qualify for the "safe" label? That's an excellent question. How about bonds? You may have been told bonds, or bond funds of any type, are safe. That is not necessarily the case. The inverse relationship of bond prices to interest rates (described earlier in this book) can cause the value of bonds to move down when interest rates rise. So, bonds and bond funds can, and do, lose money, especially in an expanding interest rate environment.

It is also a myth that corporate bonds, preferred stock and utilities are without risk. They can all lose money, and do from time to time. Safe tools are those that contractually *cannot* lose money. You will only find these in three places:

BANKS – Banks are not necessarily safe from all risk, since banks can fail. Bank accounts, however, are protected up to a point by the Federal Deposit Insurance Corporation (FDIC) and are safe up to that point.

GOVERNMENT – Government bonds are safe if you are holding the actual bonds themselves, not bond funds. These can include Treasury bonds, savings bonds, inflation bonds, savings bonds, inflation bonds, GNMAs (Government National Mortgage Association bonds, better known as Ginny Mae) and FNMAs (Federal National Mortgage Association bonds, better known as Fannie Mae). The government backs them, and the government is the only entity we know of that can print money.

INSURANCE COMPANIES – Safe financial instruments offered by insurance companies include life insurance policies and *fixed* and *fixed index* annuities, **not variable** annuities. Essentially, guarantees offered by insurance companies are subject to the claims-paying ability and financial strength of the issuing company. Can insurance companies make bad investments and go belly up? Sure, they can. So, it's always a good idea to check with an independent rating organization to determine the stability of the insurance company's financials before investing. But they are heavily regulated by the states in which they operate.

Mistake #3: Failure to Guarantee an Income

Unless you are independently wealthy to the point that money means nothing to you, and you can use $100 bills to light your cigars, your main concern in retirement will be income. Let's face it—when you were working you probably knew what your income would be each month, each year. Were you one of those people who had a monthly budget? Did you write down everything you spent so you could see at the end of the month if you were over or under budget? Or were you the type who could keep it all in your head? Either way, income was the driving factor for how much you spent.

There's an old saying, "If your outgo exceeds your income then your upkeep may be your downfall."

It is a mistake not to guarantee a substantial portion of your income in retirement. Uncle Sam guarantees a part of it—Social Security. Pensions, although they are fading from the retirement picture, are guaranteed. They are being replaced by non-guaranteed retirement plans such as 401(k)s and 403(b)s. If these qualified retirement plans use the stock market as their base (and the vast majority of them do), then they are subject to the unpredictability of that market. Upon retirement, one can continue withdrawing the same amount each month from these plans to replace the old paycheck. While that makes income predictable, there is no guarantee it will last for the rest of your life, like pensions and Social Security. As we withdraw money, we reduce the balance. While we are doing that, the market continues to surge and plunge. We love the surges, and we dread the plunges—especially in retirement. You can't feel secure about your nest egg when you park it where it can be dropped, cracked or broken.

When you plan for this phase of your life, at least a substantial portion of your income should be locked-in, down-in-writing, chiseled-in-stone guaranteed, not *proposed* or *projected*. It should flow consistently for your lifetime regardless of what the stock market does.

The reason we list this as a key mistake in retirement is that we have seen its consequences up close. We have seen happy couples, cruising through their retirement, happy as clams, not a care in the world, looking like those couples you see on the covers of senior magazines—smiling, healthy, full of life. Then the stock market collapses and wipes out half their life's savings—all because they failed to guarantee their incomes.

The market crash of 2008 was a good example of this. Some people without guaranteed incomes got what we call a "double whammy." Their portfolio values dropped because of sudden downturn and, to make matters worse, they had to continue pulling money from their investment accounts for living expenses.

Those individuals found their assets diminishing at an alarming rate.

How do you guarantee your income? Simple. You just put enough money in guaranteed strategies to deliver you the base income level that you need. Use risk accounts for the rest of your assets if you choose. But your base is always there.

Times Are Changing

Times are changing in the financial services world. Decades ago, many financial advisors were limited when it came to income planning. Their toolboxes were limited to stock-market-based and other risky financial products, or annuities with unacceptable options. Annuities in the old days were inflexible when it came to survivorship provisions. Sure, you could turn a sum of money into an income that would pay a guaranteed amount for the rest of your life, but what if you died a few months after the payout began? The insurance company kept the money. Your account balance did not go to your heirs. Those products were not flying off the shelves.

Annuities Get a Makeover

Insurance companies, like banks and other financial institutions, would be out of business if it weren't for customers. Customers vote with their pocketbooks and companies pay attention to changes in the public mood.

If you are a baby boomer, you probably remember when all Detroit could produce were big gas-guzzlers with tailfins. Then Japanese imports began eating their lunch, and the American automakers came back with fuel-efficient cars that were better built. There was even a memorable slogan from that era—"It's not your father's Oldsmobile." In the 1950s, Oldsmobiles were huge and got around 10 miles per gallon. That was okay when gasoline cost 30 cents per gallon. The buying public revolted when gas prices quintupled, and the Oldsmobile had to be redesigned. The buying public demanded it.

The insurance industry also paid attention to the mood of the American public regarding annuities in the late 1990s, when they completely retooled the annuity concept. Annuities are insurance contracts that promise a future income with money set aside to-day. The term annuity comes from the Latin word for "year." The original idea was to take a lump sum now and turn it into a yearly payout later.

Prior to its makeover, the only way to turn your lump sum into a guaranteed lifetime income was to "annuitize" the contract. But once you annuitized the contract, you couldn't pass the remainder of the money in the annuity (the amount not taken as income) on to your heirs. Take the income and die early, and the insurance company kept what was not paid out.

The new-style annuities no longer required you to annuitize to create a lifetime income. That meant you could now exercise the income option and pass along whatever was left in the account, along with the gains, to your heirs. Baby boomers began paying attention. According to LIMRA, a life insurance market research association, "In 2016, total fixed annuity sales hit a record-breaking $117.4 billion, 14 percent higher than 2015 levels." [67]

Annuities are not for everyone. You likely shouldn't put money into one if you think you will need those assets for daily living expenses in the near future. The annuity company assumes you will not need the money you put into the annuity until you retire. But since emergencies do arise, most insurance companies have a provision that allows you to withdraw 10 percent of your balance every year, if you deem it necessary, without paying a penalty.

---

[67] ThinkAdvisor. Feb. 21, 2017. "Fixed annuity sales hit record $117.4 billion in 2016." http://www.thinkadvisor.com/2017/02/21/fixed-annuity-sales-hit-record-1174-billion-in-201.

Withdrawals of more than that will usually incur a penalty called a "surrender charge." These charges can range from 6 percent to 14 percent, depending on the terms of your contract. Surrender charges typically decrease each year you keep the contract until they reach zero. The customary surrender period for retirement annuities is around 10 years.

Income Riders

How do income riders work? Riders are to insurance contracts what options are to automobiles. But the option of an income rider has become so significant of late that few are sold without them. Not all income riders are alike and there are several moving parts, but the principle is the same. You can get a guaranteed lifetime income stream without having to annuitize.

An income rider is purchased at a fee deducted from the balance of the account each year. With annuities whose gains are predicated on the performance of a market index (fixed index annuities), the fee for the income rider, which is typically 1 percent or less, is deducted from the gains. In a year where the market declines, the return is zero, and the fee is deducted from the account balance.

Insurance companies work with a formula when it comes to the payout. They factor in the age of the annuitant and the income account value. With these products, the *income account value* is not the same as the actual *contract value.* The two grow at different rates. The *income account* usually has a crediting method applied to it by the insurance company and typically grows by anywhere from 4 percent to 8 percent per year as long as the income is not taken. Once the income is triggered, the growth in the income account stops, but the income continues for life.

Mistake #4: Not Paying Attention to <u>All</u> Your Portfolio Costs

The old-fashioned "buy-and-hold" strategy promoted as gospel by many investment counselors for years doesn't work well in volatile markets. This has led to an increase in the number of actively managed accounts. But actively managed accounts generate a side effect—trading fees. Reacting quickly to ever-changing market conditions is expensive. Each trade the manager logs in costs money, and this can cause a drag on the performance of the account. Depending on the level of activity, it can be like driving a car with one foot on the gas pedal and one foot on the brake.

Hidden Expenses

As pointed out in Chapter Four of this book, the investment world is full of hidden expenses. Mutual funds top the list, but they certainly are not alone. A March 1, 2010, article in the *Wall Street Journal* titled "The Hidden Cost of Mutual Funds" said Americans who own mutual funds pay an average of 1.31 percent each year to the portfolio manager and for other operating expenses.

"But that's not the real bottom line," the article said. "There are other costs, not reported in the expense ratio, related to the buying and selling of securities in the portfolio, and those expenses can make a fund two or three times as costly…"

The average investor just shrugs and proclaims the expense too difficult to figure out. Why bother trying to understand something so complex? What you want to ask yourself is *when was the last time you've had a truly objective analysis done on your portfolio expenses, disclosed and hidden?* You deserve to have this information if it applies to your situation. You deserve to be able to understand documents associated with your investments so you can ferret out hidden commissions and fees.

Mistake #5: Mistaking Your Tax Preparer for a Tax Planner

You customarily see your tax preparer once each year prior to April 15. It is a common misconception that those few minutes you spend discussing tax forms with your accountant is tax planning. No, what you are doing there is trying to make sure the right numbers go in the proper boxes to make the IRS happy. It is a useful and necessary activity, but it is not tax planning.

Tax planning requires taking full advantage of every opportunity the IRS affords you to avoid paying unnecessary taxes. The reason most tax preparation specialists don't do this is because they are not trained to provide that kind of guidance. It is not in their wheelhouse to spot how your assets may be positioned so you don't pay more than your fair share to Uncle Sam. Tax planners typically work hand in glove with your financial advisor.

Common Areas of Over-Taxation

Here are some common areas on your tax return where you may be paying more to the IRS than you have to:

- Tax on phantom income (paying tax on income that you don't use)
- Unnecessary taxes on your Social Security income (you already paid tax on this as the money went into the system, and now you have to pay again as it comes out?)
- Double tax on IRA distributions
- Phantom tax on municipal bond interest (wasn't this supposed to be tax free?)
- Tax on non-retirement account income (this can often be structured to be 90% tax-free)

Phantom Income

Phantom income is income reported as having been paid to a taxpayer but was not actually received. If you own stocks, for example, and you sell shares of those stocks at a profit but do not withdraw those profits from the account, you still owe taxes on the gains within your account. Another example is zero-coupon bonds, which are issued at a discount and mature at par. The interest payments are credited to you but no actual check is cut. If you own one of these bonds, the money doesn't actually go into your pocket until you redeem the bond at the highest par value.

Social Security Tax

We call this the "senior-only tax," because only those who are collecting Social Security pay it. Depending on their income picture, many pay it because of lack of planning. If your tax preparer is just filling in the boxes, he or she will probably not inform you there are perfectly legitimate and legal ways to avoid paying this unnecessary tax. Every situation is different, but your financial advisor should know what to do with this one. See Chapter Five of this book for possible solutions to this problem.

Double Tax on IRA Distributions After Death

Without tax planning, the estate will be hit with taxes when the owner of an IRA dies, and then, when your heirs begin taking their required minimum distributions (RMDs) from the IRA account. They will have to pay ordinary income tax on the amounts that are distributed. Hence the term, "double tax." Failure to track what is called "basis" in an IRA can also cause you tax heartaches. A competent financial advisor should be able to help you avoid this train wreck, if possible.

Municipal Bond Interest

Always ask questions when you hear the words "tax-free." There are all kinds of taxes—state tax, federal tax, corporation tax, income tax, sales tax, gasoline tax, property tax. U.S. government bonds are free from state and local taxes. Municipal bonds are free from federal taxes, and may be free from state taxes, as well, if you buy bonds issued by the state you live in.

Traditional bonds pay annual interest, which is normally taxed. The lack of interest payments does not prevent a holder of zero-coupon bonds from avoiding tax, however. The bondholder will be presented with a statement of **imputed** interest. This is sometimes referred to as **phantom interest.** This amount is based on the eventual realized gain broken down over the life of the bond. This imputed interest is then taxed each year, just like traditional bond interest. There are municipal bonds sold as zero-coupon bonds and like traditional municipal bonds, the imputed interest can be free of federal taxes. Zero coupon bonds don't pay interest but are sold at a deep discount from their face value. As a bond nears maturity, it increases in value. At maturity, you get the full face value. The drawback of a zero-coupon bond is you have to pay annual taxes on "phantom" income (price appreciation) while you are holding it. A tax planning session with a qualified financial advisor may just help you avoid unnecessary taxation in this arena as well.

Tax-Free Income

Is tax-free income possible? Is it legal? Yes to both. Uncle Sam giveth with his right hand and taketh away with his left. Fair or not, the government makes the rules and, if you are a citizen of the United States of America, then one of the privileges you have is playing in the game and doing your fair share.

It is unlikely you will ever understand all the provisions of the Internal Revenue Code. The complete IRC contains 74,608 pages, according to an April 15, 2017 article in the *Washington Examiner.* It contains more than 4 million words, according to Kelly Phillips in *Forbes* magazine! It is full of sections and chapters and subchapters and subsections. But paid professionals are at your service who make it their business to keep up with what laws and provisions within the IRC pertain to you and your estate. Entire computer programs are devoted to enabling searches through this complex and exhausting set of laws.[68, 69]

Who would you say pays the most in taxes? Those who plan and are informed, or those who fail to plan and are not informed? The latter, of course.

Mistake # 6: Not Seeing the Tax Implications of Qualified Accounts

Any plan that meets the requirements of the Internal Revenue Code and is eligible to receive certain tax benefits is called a "qualified" account. You may know them better as IRAs, 401(k)s, 403(b)s, etc. Under the terms of a 401(k), for example, you pay no tax on the money as you contribute it toward the plan. The contribution is deducted from your paycheck and credited to your 401(k) account. The contribution is not considered "reportable" income by the IRS. Great, right? Well, yes and no. Uncle Sam has given you two choices—pay me now or pay me later. Unless it is a Roth IRA or 401(k), you have chosen to pay him later.

Think of it this way. You are a farmer buying seed for planting season. You are in the seed store and a man dressed up like Uncle Sam comes up to you and says, "I'll make you a deal, Partner. Pay no taxes whatsoever on the seed you are buying, but go ahead and plant it, and I will tax you on the harvest instead."

You would turn him down flat, wouldn't you? Yet, that is just what qualified plans do. You pay no money on the money you contribute to the plan, or while your money is growing. But you

---

[68] Jason Russell. Washington Examiner. April 15, 2016. "Look at how many pages are in the federal tax code." http://www.washingtonexaminer.com/look-at-how-many-pages-are-in-the-federal-tax-code/article/2563032.

[69] Kelly Phillips Erb. Forbes. Jan. 10, 2013. "Tax Code Hits Nearly 4 Million Words." https://www.forbes.com/sites/kellyphillipserb/2013/01/10/tax-code-hits-nearly-4-million-words-taxpayer-advocate-calls-it-too-complicated/#18a7ceab6e24.

will pay taxes on the money you withdraw at your current tax rate.

Here are some basic things you need to know about qualified accounts:

Every dollar you take out is taxed.

Remember, we are dealing with the government here. Why would they be interested in giving you a tax deferment? They know that over time, those skinny dollars going in will fatten, earning them more taxes in the long run. Even when you die and pass along your IRA to heirs, Uncle Sam will either get his taxes all at once, if your heirs take a full distribution (not a good idea, by the way), or get it later after the account has grown even fatter. The government is in no hurry. Remember, it can print money. Deferred taxation is one of the smartest ideas Congress ever came up with.

Withdrawals can be more expensive than you think.

Let's say an unexpected situation pops up requiring you to shell out some major bucks. It could be anything from a buying opportunity on some rental property you can't afford to pass up, a health problem, or a new roof. You don't have the money in your checking account. You don't have enough in checking or savings, and you don't want to use a credit card. Then you remember the thousands of dollars you have tucked away in a qualified account. You decide to withdraw a chunk of that money. Since it is a qualified money, the custodian of the account is required to report the withdrawal to the IRS. You will receive a 1099 as if you were paid the money as a contract worker. If you are under 59 ½, you will likely owe 10 percent in addition to income taxes on the money withdrawn. In the end, you will lose several ways. In addition to paying penalty and taxes, you lose the potential interest the account could have earned had you left it alone. In some situations, it is wiser to borrow money than to withdraw it from a qualified account.

What if you are receiving Social Security income, and you withdraw funds from a qualified account? The IRS treats it as ordinary income, No. 1. And, No. 2, depending on how you have your income structured, it could be just enough to kick you into the bracket where you must now pay taxes on either 50 percent or 85 percent of your Social Security. That will depend, of course, on your **total reportable** annual income. Your financial advisor should be able to walk you through this and determine where you stand and how such a withdrawal would affect you.

Required minimum distributions eventually come into play. The IRS will not allow you to defer taxes on a qualified account forever. The law requires you to begin making withdrawals and paying taxes on those withdrawals beginning April 1 of the year following the year in which you turn age 70 ½. If you are like most people, you did not dwell too deeply about what you would be doing when you hit your 70s. You were too busy building a career, having fun with your young friends, perhaps raising a family. Meanwhile, the money in your qualified retirement account continued growing (hopefully). Let's say you eventually succeed financially to the point where you really don't need to pull money from your IRAs or other qualified accounts. You just want to leave it to your heirs. Sorry, Charlie. Uncle Sam's rules won't let you. Whether you need the money or not, and whether you wish to do it or not, you will be forced to take those RMDs and pay taxes on it. The percentage is not a killer, but it increases as each year goes by (if you decide not to take your RMD, you will owe 50 percent of that year's RMD you were supposed to take to the IRS). You can estimate your RMD by dividing your year-end IRA balance by the number of years of your life expectancy. You may use the tables given in Appendix C of IRS Publication 590, Individual Retirement Arrangements, or you may consult your financial planner when you have that tax-planning session.

Mistake #7: Not Knowing How Much Liquidity They Need

It is a financial fact of life: you can either have money, or you have what money will buy... but you can't have both at the same time. Once you spend a dollar, *that* dollar is gone forever. You may replace it with *another* dollar in time, but *that* dollar is gone.

Liquidity is here-and-now money, easily accessed with the stroke of a pen or the push of a button. Many treasure the notion of having immediate and total control over their cash, so much so that they keep an extraordinary amount of it in low-yielding accounts, such as money markets or certificates of deposit at the bank. So, it's a matter of tradeoffs. Immediate and easy access to your money will cost you in growth potential. It's a matter of trade-offs. Seldom will you find the "big three"—safety of principal, growth potential and liquidity—hanging out at the same counter. Every investment option we know of gives you two of those features, and you have to sacrifice the third to get the other two. For example, a mutual fund is liquid and has growth potential, but you sacrifice a measure of safety. CDs give you liquidity and safety of principal, but you sacrifice growth potential.

The main reason retirees desire liquidity is fear of the unknown. Even wealthy investors tend to park too much money in low-yielding savings accounts and money market funds as retirement approaches.

Fear is the main cause for the desire for liquidity—the fear of unexpected expenses, the fear of stock market volatility. Even wealthy Americans tend to park too much of their money in low-yield savings accounts, CDs and money market funds as they approach retirement. They may complain about the returns but insist on complete control of their cash. That was the consensus of a 2010 poll taken by Harris Interactive and sponsored by MetLife. Pollsters surveyed 1,858 Americans age 45 and older, including 500 people with between $200,000 and $1 million in investable assets. Among those with more than $200,000 in investable assets, half reported having at least one unexpected expense in the past year that cost $2,000, and 29 percent had between two and five such expenses. To them, accepting lower returns was seen as a way to ensure the safety of their money and maintain fast access to their funds.[70]

The unexpected expenses were not always their own. Many of those surveyed said they felt they had to care for not only their own emergency needs but those of younger and older family members. Half of all those surveyed in the MetLife poll said they would be comfortable giving up access to a portion of their retirement savings in order to receive the most income possible. The other half said it was more important to them to have complete control of their retirement savings at *all* times, even if it means less income in the long run.

So, what is the solution? Education. Knowledge dispels fear. A competent financial advisor will be able to help retirees determine appropriate liquidity, find ways to achieve it using modern financial products, and put the rest of their assets to work.

Let's say you have $500,000 in your retirement portfolio. How much of that will you need to access at any one time? Only you can determine the answer. Every situation is different. But most retirees we work with don't wish to invade their principal. They just want to take earnings if they can. They like the idea of protecting their nest egg and living off the interest, if possible.

---

[70] Ruthie Ackerman. FinancialPlanning. Nov. 18, 2010. "Meeting Clients Needs: Liquidity Versus Retirement Savings." https://www.financial-planning.com/news/meeting-clients-needs-liquidity-versus-retirement-savings.

Generally, there are three circumstances for which retirees need immediate access to their money:

- A major purchase, such as a new car or another home. Usually this is done with money outside their core nest egg.
- Helping their children. Some retirees may wish to help out their children with business ventures, support them in a financial crisis, or help with college funding for grandchildren.
- Health care. Unexpected health care costs increase as people get older.

With careful planning, you can strike a balance and retire with security and adequate liquidity.

Mistake #8: Collecting Social Security Too Early

We covered much of this in Chapter Six of this book, but it deserves repeating. We hear this question a lot: "At what age should I begin taking my Social Security?" We realize they probably want a straight answer. Unfortunately, we can't give them one. The answer is, "it depends."

The government says you can begin taking your Social Security as early as age 62. And that's true. But you can wait until age 70 and collect more per month. So, what to do? If you collect as early as allowed by law, your benefits could be reduced by 25-30 percent. For most baby boomers, full retirement age is 66. Yes, you receive what the Social Security Administration calls "full benefits" if you wait until full retirement age, but if you wait even longer, and you receive an extra 8 percent per year for each extra working year up to age 70.

Here again, there is no one-size-fits-all. Factors you might want to consider:

- Your health. If you have serious health concerns that could lead to a shorter life expectancy, perhaps it is to your financial advantage to start collecting your benefits earlier.
- Your income. If you are still working, and you collect Social Security, the government can reduce your payments.
- Your marital status. Collection strategies vary if you are married, divorced or widowed. Depending on the exact details, you could benefit from collecting early or waiting as long as possible.

Like we said—it all depends on your situation. When and how to collect Social Security can be a complicated process. Competent financial advisors can walk you through it, however, and help you decide what is most advantageous for you.

"But will Social Security still be there for me when I retire?" is a question we hear quite often. If you are a baby boomer (born between 1946 and 1964), the answer is almost certainly yes, according to a report published in 2015 by Tom Anderson, personal finance writer for CNBC. According to Anderson, lack of confidence in the future of the Social Security system is one of the main reasons why people claim their benefits early. He points out:

"Social Security Administration forecasts that its trust fund for retirement benefits will be exhausted by 2034. However, even if Congress does nothing to shore up one of the nation's most popular federal programs, the Social Security Administration projects it will have enough money from payroll taxes to cover three-quarters of retirement benefits promised to retirees through 2090." [71]

---

[71] Tom Anderson. CNBC. Aug. 26, 2015. "Retirees pay for claiming Social Security too early." http://www.cnbc.com/2015/08/26/retirees-pay-for-claiming-social-security-too-early.html.

CHAPTER ELEVEN

The Planning Process—the Way It Should Be Done

"Planning ahead is a matter of class. The rich and even the middle class plan for future generations, but the poor can plan ahead for only a few weeks or days."

~ *Gloria Steinem*

A couple came to our office one morning for an interview. It was right after the stock market had plunged precipitously, wiping out a sizable chunk of their retirement savings. Their faces showed deep concern as they told us their story.

Considering their ages (both were 63), and their proximity to retirement, their financial advisor had them too heavily weighted in risky growth stocks. They said they wished they had paid more attention, but they were too busy with their careers, and thought they were "all taken care of" when it came to their investments.

They had planned to retire when they reached 65. They had dreams of traveling. Her grandmother was Italian by birth, and she had collected brochures of all the places they wanted to see in the "old country." He loved tinkering with antique cars and looked forward to when he would have the time to restore a 1967 Mustang that sat covered by a tarp in a shed beside their home.

Those plans would have to be put on hold. With their retirement savings reduced by more than one third, their target date for retirement would have to be postponed.

"Don't worry about the market," their financial advisor had told them. "It always bounces back."

Of course, their financial advisor was right. Historically, when the stock market takes a tumble, it has always come back. But this couple was on the cusp of retirement. Would they have time to wait on the recovery? It was doubtful.

Timing is critical when it comes to managing our wealth for retirement. As we have pointed out in this book time and time again, having too much at risk as retirement approaches can put your entire retirement at risk.

Financial planning can be fraught with dangers similar to those that beset this couple if you do not have competent guidance. All too often, you don't realize you need guidance until you find you have made a wrong turn. Choosing a guide may be the most important financial decision you make in your life.

Trust plays a crucial role in selecting a financial advisor. That is why so many people turn to relatives and friends. That's what this couple had done. They selected a financial advisor based on the recommendation of a family member.

DIY Investing

The two areas of life where you should not take a do-it-yourself approach are your **health** and your **wealth.** We know of individuals who use any excuse not to visit a doctor. Their pattern is to wait for a pain that can't be dismissed by aspirin before they give in and seek medical attention. Some of these folks are no longer with us and would still be alive had they not procrastinated seeking professional help.

No one we know of would attempt self-dentistry or self-surgery. But there are those who attempt do-it-yourself financial planning. A little trading on the side with money you can afford to lose is one thing. But plunging into the market on your own with your life's savings is flirting with disaster. That's why we recommend leaving financial planning to professionals. Sure, some people we know have learned quite a bit about technical analysis and have learned how to move in and out of positions in the stock market and have done pretty well, all things considered. But they are in the minority. Most who try do-it-yourself investing fail miserably because their emotions get in the way, and they try to time the market, chasing hot stock tips and rumors.

We saw a cartoon right after the tech bubble burst in 2000, depicting a sad-faced man dressed in a tattered business suit, standing on a street corner, holding up a hand-lettered sign that read: "Need Money to Continue Day Trading." Millions of Americans have lost millions of dollars through the lure of online trading.

Choosing the Right Advisor for You

If we have made any point in this book, it is that every person and every financial situation is different. Selecting the right financial advisor for you may require some legwork on your part to assure yourself an candidate is a fit for your unique circumstance.

The interview process is key. Ask questions. True professionals will welcome your inquiries. They will be happy to tell you about their training and the designations that have earned that represent their expertise and experience. They will be just as interested in getting to know you, too.

Ask this trick question: "*What is your investing philosophy?*"

A trustworthy advisor will probably not answer quickly. A competent advisor will need more information about *you* before offering *you* an investing strategy or concept. If you ask that question of a true professional, you will likely get questions in return. What is your time horizon, your income needs, your tax situation, how is your current portfolio invested, and many others. Just like a doctor will ask you what medications you are allergic to before offering you a prescription, the right advisor for you will get to know you before making any recommendations.

Good Communication

Good communication between you and your advisor is a must. You will want to know who your contact person at the office will be. How often will you talk to them? Who else will be on your team? Will it include one of the firm's principals?

Ask how the firm is paid. That's not a personal question; that's a business question. Competent professionals will be transparent in this regard. How financial advisors are compensated may reveal much about their level of objectivity. For example, Registered Investment Advisors generally work on a fee-only or fee-plus commission basis. A "fee-only" financial advisor will work by the hour or will charge a flat fee. Many advisors charge a percentage of the assets they manage in your behalf. This means the advisor is rewarded for growing your portfolio. The flat-rate or hourly fees usually come with a one-time service the advisor renders, such as developing a financial plan. Some advisors receive a portion of the commissions involved when a client buys or subscribes to a particular financial product, such as an insurance policy or annuity. This may be apart from fees or in addition to fees, but usually does not come out of the clients' pockets.

A travel agency is paid commissions, for example. When you book a flight or a hotel through a travel agency, you expect them to save you money and provide you with a better-quality trip than if you made your own arrangements. But you never pay them a dime. The travel agent should be able to shop for the best fares and accommodations for you, and your itinerary will be tailor-made to suit you. Who pays them? They are compensated by the hotels and airlines. There's nothing wrong with that as long as you are the ultimate benefactor.

No financial advisor works free of charge. If they tell you that, run for the exits, because anything else they tell you is of questionable veracity. Profit and remuneration are not dirty words in the free enterprise system. Neither is "commission" a dirty word. But make sure you are dealing with a fiduciary. True fiduciaries are not obligated to offer any one product or service. They are not beholden to a company. They are independent and are legally obligated to make recommendations that are only in your best interest, irrespective of what they are paid.

No One-Size-Fits-All

Picture yourself walking into a high-end department store to buy a quality pair of shoes. You are greeted by a salesperson.

"How may I help you?" he says.

"I need to buy a pair of shoes—size 10 ½," you say.

"Oh, we only have one size here—size 9," he says.

Ridiculous, right? Of course! Why would you not settle for a size and a half smaller than the size your feet require? You wouldn't. It defies logic and reason. Even if the size offered you were marked size 10 ½, you would try them on first and make sure they fit you. To do otherwise, and try to walk in them, could be hazardous to your health.

That well illustrates how ridiculous it would be to sign up for a cookie-cutter financial plan that is not custom-fitted for you and you alone. Financially speaking, you are unique. That is the central point we hope we have made in this book. Just as every individual has a separate and distinct physical fingerprint, each of us has a unique set of financial circumstances and economic drivers that characterize us.

With that nail firmly in the plank, please allow us one more strike of the hammer to drive home this one last point. Like a good pair of shoes or a well-tailored suit, a financial plan will just fit you, and you will know it immediately, just like you know your right shoe is on your right foot. No one has to tell you that. You just know. If it doesn't match your unique financial circumstances—your hopes, wishes, dreams and plans for the future—then it is not for you. The financial advisors who are right for *you* will know how important that is to you without having to be told.

Made in the USA
Columbia, SC
12 February 2018